Dedication

I'm super excited to dedicate this book to my amazing son Eli because without him, it probably wouldn't have happened. I'm a procrastinator when it comes to doing things I don't love, and I don't love to write. Eli said, "Dad, you just have to commit to working on it for one hour every day. I will hold you accountable." For the past six months, I've woken up at five a.m. and done exactly that. Every Friday, Eli got up with me and I read him everything I had written that week. He gave me feedback and suggestions from the perspective of a fourth grader. He's probably listened to me read each chapter fifteen times and is excited to read and see the reviews y'all leave on Amazon (so be kind). Eli, thank you for being a kind, compassionate, loving son and big brother. I am so proud to be your dad. Also to my daughter, Brooklyn, and son Cameron (CJ). I love you three more than you know and try my hardest to be the best daddy to you. To my beautiful wife, Renee, thank you for being the perfect mommy to our kids. Without your support and understanding, it would be impossible for me to have the career I do. I am the luckiest man in the world.

D1452113

The Teacher Learning Center is proud to provide exceptional staff development services in the areas of classroom and behavior management, school discipline, S.E.L., and student/staff motivation to school districts all over the world.

Follow Brian:
Twitter: @brianmendler
Instagram: @brianmendler
Facebook: @brianmendlerfanpage
YouTube: https://www.youtube.com/c/brianmendler
Podcast: The Brian Mendler Show

To contact Brian for keynotes, institutes, on-site or virtual trainings call 833-572-4900 or email info@tlc-seminars.com.

This book is available at special discounts when purchased in quantity for educational purposes or for the use of promotions or fundraisers. For inquiries and details, contact the publisher at info@tlc-seminars.com.

Teacher
Learning
Center

Printed in the United States of America.
Cover Design by Blue Water Printing, Rochester, NY

TABLE OF
CONTENTS

Introduction

D an was seated to my left and Mike was directly across from me. There was an empty desk next to Dan. They were arranged in a horseshoe shape, and I sat in my black rolling chair at the opening, facilitating a discussion on the Civil War. This was one of my favorite topics, as it generated heated but engaging comments. Both kids were known to be volatile. With me privately, Mike was working on walking away from arguments and fights when he felt angry. He was allowed, without asking, to go to Mr. Kilgore's office (the social worker attached to our self-contained program) two doors down. Dan didn't know Mike was working on this, as I'm a firm believer in not sharing people's business with everyone. As the discussion progressed, I noticed Dan's leg started shaking; a telltale sign he was getting aggravated. Mike was arguing his point, and without hesitation, quickly picked himself up to leave. Dan, believing Mike was coming toward him, jumped over the desk and punched him. I grabbed Dan by the back of his green Nike hooded sweatshirt and pulled. He stumbled backward, turned around, picked me up by my shirt collar, and threw me onto a desk. Anthony, a six-foot-three, two-hundred-pound football player ran full speed across the room and tackled Dan yelling, "What are you doing? You can't hit a teacher! Are you crazy?"

Dan snapped out of his rage. "Oh my gosh. Mr. Mendler, I'm so sorry. I would never try to hurt you. I'm so sorry." He crumbled to the floor and sobbed uncontrollably. Dan was suspended for a few days. The day he returned, he walked into my room with his hat pulled low, hood up, staring at the ground. He sat quietly that day, and at the end of class said to me, "Mr. Mendler, I'm sorry. Sometimes I lose control of myself. It's like I black out, but I have medication now that will help."

I said, "That's great, but if this happens on the street with someone random, there can be serious trouble."

He said, "I know, I get it, and I promise things are going to change. I'm sorry." We shook hands as we had done many times in the past. Almost to the door, he turned, looked me directly in the eye and said, "Mr. Mendler, you were kind of light. I picked you up easily. If you want, I'll stay after school and work out with you," and ran out.

The incident with Dan was the first and only time in my career I felt completely lost. Obviously, it's never okay for a student to put hands on a teacher. What Dan did was unacceptable, and there was no excuse. That said, one of the most important concepts of this book is that changing the behavior of a kid always starts with changing your own behavior first. Where in the sequence of events that happened could I have possibly done or said something different to diffuse the situation? I want to be clear: I'm not saying the adult is at fault. I am saying we often play a role in the action taken by the student, and the only person we control is us. You will notice this is a theme throughout the book.

Dan's incident was the most challenging of my career, and it wasn't easy to look in the mirror after being thrown onto a desk. In retrospect, Mike should have been next to me and Dan across. I was taught that my most volatile student should be closest to me, so Dan was directly to my left. He was separated from Mike by one student and two empty desks (think horseshoe-shaped desk setup). I had prevented Dan from fighting a few times that year, each time approaching him from the front. But this time, I yanked his hood from behind and his instincts took over. If their seats were switched, when Mike had gotten up to leave, Dan would have come at Mike, but toward me instead of away. I would have gotten in front of him instead of pulling him from behind, and would have had the opportunity to say, "Hey, walk this way. Think about what you're about to do. It's not worth it," and usher him back before escalation.

Chapter One

Behaviors Are Never the Problem

D iscomfort is the appetizer for growth, both physically and emotionally. We cannot grow in this world without feeling at least a little bit of it first. Usually our instinct is to run from the discomfort, and hide and get as far away from it as we possibly can.

December 23, 2001 was the most uncomfortable day of my life. I'll never forget my first addiction recovery meeting. I walked in more terrified than I've felt for anything. I was so scared that I looked into the room and decided not to go. This is how sick many addicts are. We don't think about eight steps ahead in life. We think about what feels best for me at this moment. What felt best for me was to turn and run because I instinctively run and hide from discomfort. I had done it my whole life and was about to do it again.

As I turned to leave, I ran smack into a man standing behind me. His name was Kevin. I bounced right off of him as our eyes locked. I immediately looked away and took one giant step around him. As I did so, I felt a hand grab my arm. I looked, and it was him. In the calmest voice you could ever imagine, he said, "You look like an addict. Come with me," and pulled me into the room.

Every time I tell that story, I pause and look at the sky to say thank you. I'm forty-six years old, and in forty-six years on this planet, being pulled into that room by that man that night is the greatest thing that's ever happened in my life, and that says something because I have a pretty great life. I have an amazing career. I have three beautiful children that I love more than anything. My son Eli just finished fourth grade. My daughter, Brooklyn, finished second grade, and my son Cameron is sixteen months old. She hates when I say it, but my wife is a world-renowned abstract artist with over 73 thousand followers on Instagram (@reneemendlerart). But despite all the great things in my life, the best thing that could have happened to me was being pulled into that room by that man that night. Because without my recovery, I would not have my kids. I would not have my wife, and I definitely would not have this career.

However, something very comforting for me in my life is knowing that even without my kids, wife, and career, I still have my recovery. It's something nobody can take from me. It also means my recovery always comes first in my life. When I taught kids full time, they had a homework assignment every Monday. Their job was to enter class on Tuesday and ask how my recovery meeting went Monday night for no other reason but to hold me accountable. Want to get a bunch of disruptive, unmotivated kids to start caring? Here's an idea I guarantee some of you haven't tried: figure out a way for them to take care of you.

We spend so much time taking care of kids, and rightfully so, but think about it from the reverse perspective. When a person lives their entire life being helped, it's easy to become helpless. That's what helplessness is. When we flip this and the helped become the helpers, we often see a major shift in many kids.

Tuesdays were always my favorite days to teach. From fifteen different angles, I'd hear, "Mr. Mendler, you went last night, right?" "Hey, Mr. Mendler, did you go last night?" "Mr. Mendler, how was your meeting last night?" "Mr. Mendler, is there anything you learned last night you can teach us?" In twenty years of attending recovery meetings, I've never been to one where I haven't learned multiple things I could teach my students the next day.

I'll give you an example of one right now. In recovery, we have a phrase called "the windshield." The windshield is a reminder that in life, you have to go forward. You may want to look back at where you came from, but if you drive a car and stare in the rear view mirror, you will crash every time. Rear view mirrors are not made for staring; they are made for glancing. This phrase has never been truer than it is right now. Kids have always stared at negative things. Something their parents did. Something someone said about them on the computer. Something their boyfriend or girlfriend did. That's always been a thing, and still is. It's nice to have a phrase reminding each other to go forward.

There was another man in the room that night named Chris. He sat at the head of a long, rectangular table. It was obvious he was in charge. He looked at me for a moment before asking, "What's your name, and why are you here?"

"My name is Brian, and I'm here because I have a bad problem with gambling," I replied.

"No you don't," he said definitively.

Annoyed, I said, "Excuse me? Yes I do."

"No. You don't. The biggest misconception people have when they come to addiction recovery is they believe the addiction is their problem," Chris explained. That's what I thought because that's what everybody always said. Chris continued, "Brian? Hide your purse. Brian? Hide your wallet. Brian has a drug problem. Brian has a gambling problem. Oh no, here comes Brian." He paused and looked at me before saying, "I want to be first to tell you that gambling is not your problem, it's the solution you've chosen to your problems and there's a good chance you don't know what your real problems are. Do me a favor and close your eyes real quick."

So I did. He said, "Imagine a big pile of snow or dirt. Got it? Every time you use, it's like you grab a shovel, walk over to that pile of snow or dirt, pick up a huge scoop, walk over to your problems, and dump it right on them because you don't want to face them. In these rooms, we help you dig out problems, force you to face them, and then teach you how to handle them with new solutions. Are you interested?"

Was I ever? All of a sudden, this man I had never met before separated the addiction from me and put it into the stratosphere. Then he said, "And, Brian, one last thing. If you never come back to another meeting in your life, I don't really care, but please remember this rule: in life, adults make choices and children make excuses. No more excuses."

I tell you all of this for two reasons. First, as I started talking about my addiction, I've learned that addiction is sort of like cancer in the sense that you've either had it yourself or know someone very close who has. So hopefully for someone reading or listening, I can be an inspiration, but that's not really why I tell you this. The real reason I tell you this is I work with schools all the time—149 in the year 2021 to be exact—and there's a phrase that I often hear educators use. The phrase drives me crazy, and it's always driven me crazy, but I never said anything because I always felt like if I said something, I had to go "all in" and tell my whole story or not touch it at all. I never felt comfortable telling my whole story, so I never touched it. But since I just told my whole story, now I get to touch it. That phrase is "behavior problems." You hear it all the time:

"You got that kid in your class? He's known to have a behavior problem."

"Oh her? She's a never ending behavior problem."

"I taught his sister three years ago and she had a behavior problem too."

"I taught his mom nineteen years ago and could've predicted it then!"

I'd like to be the first to tell you, like Chris was to tell me, from this moment forward there is no such thing as a "behavior problem" child in your school because the truth is, behavior is to kids what gambling is to me. It's not the problem, it's the solution they pick to their problems, and there's a good chance kids don't know what their real problems are. Every time they misbehave, it's like they grab a shovel, walk over to that pile of snow or dirt, pick up a huge scoop, head over to their problems, and dump it right on them because they don't want to face them. However, if you and I can help dig out their problems, force them to face them, and then teach them how to handle them with new solutions, not only will they improve, but we will change their lives. That's what this whole thing is about for me. Changing people's lives.

If you're tired, if you're confused, if you're annoyed, if you're not sure what decision to make for a kid, focus on your legacy. Focus on how you want to be thought of when it's all over, because the truth is, you have 15 days of school left, or 50 days of school left, or 100 or 180 days of school left to make sure you are properly remembered. My grandma, God bless her soul, used to say, "When they put you in the ground, they don't put anything in there with you." Her point was that material possessions don't matter. It doesn't matter what you have when you're on this earth. What does matter is if you died tomorrow, would they be lined up at your funeral? Would they have to shut down the school, the district, the town, because so many people wanted to attend, or would they say, "Good riddance, I'm glad they're gone"? The only thing that matters is what you leave behind when you're gone. She would say, "Treat every person as though someday they will be doing life-saving surgery on you." Allow all your decisions to come from the foundation of what you want others to think of you.

I quickly learned my biggest problem was always believing everyone else was the problem. This was a theme throughout my life from the time I was a little kid. When I failed a test, I justified it with the belief that the teacher was dumb and didn't know how to teach. If I got cut from a team, I'd say that the coach was an idiot and that he probably never even played a sport. If a girl didn't like me, I'd say she was clueless (although, that one might be true). Then I got into recovery and learned the single most important lesson, not just for teaching, but for my life. Every single time in my life that I have a problem with someone or something, I am at least part of the cause of that problem, and if I'm willing to change me, I will change everything around me.

In recovery, I'd say, "But that person was disrespectful."

They'd say, "Yeah, but did you have to feel disrespected?"

"Did you not hear me? I said that person was disrespectful," I'd insist.

"Yes, Brian, we heard you. We got that part, but our question is, did you have to feel disrespected? Disrespectful is about someone else. Disrespected is about you. Changing you will change everything around you."

Imagine if all kids and all adults in all schools looked at all behaviors this way. You have the kid in the red corner (not most kids, but some). You have the teacher in the blue corner (not most teachers, but some). Some kids and certain teachers seem to meet in the middle of the ring and fight every day. Wouldn't it be cool if just for one day, instead of looking at each other, they'd looked at themselves the whole walk there? By the time they'd get to the center of the ring, they'd fight each other to say "I'm sorry" first. The democrats and republicans should all come listen to me too. Imagine if just for one day, instead of yelling at each other about all the problems in our country, they'd look at themselves, and admit their mistakes:

"We wrote this article that wasn't true."

"I know, but we exaggerated that story."

"Yeah, but we knew that because we were spying on you."

"We know because we were spying on your spies." By the end, they'd all give each other big hugs.

Do you have a referral form at your school or district? If so, does it have a spot that asks what the adult did wrong? What about a spot asking what the adult can do differently next time? I believe those should be the first two questions on the form. Not because I believe adults in school are usually the problem. Please read that again. I do not believe adults in school are usually the problem. I also believe everyone should look in the mirror first. Two things can be true at the same time, but you have to admit the adult is the problem some of the time. Tell me there are not some adults in your school that are really good at pouring gasoline on a little tiny fire. There was a tiny fire, they walked over with a whole can of gasoline, and were baffled by why there was an explosion. If forced to put a number on who was at fault in a power struggle between a kid and adult, I would say 70/30 kid/adult. Since most people reading are teachers, I will be nice and say 90/10.

I have a strange superstition when I fly. I get to the airport, through security and to the gate, then I stare at the airplane. Don't ask why. I don't know anything about airplanes. I'm no aviation expert but I'm also no idiot. I can see if a wing is missing. I can see if there's a hole in the fuselage. My thing is, I'm not going down for something I should have seen. If we go down, I want to be able to look at the lady next to me and say, "I promise I looked, and it was nothing obvious." Knock on wood. Thankfully, there's never been an issue.

Imagine you start doing this, and as you look out

the window, you notice part of the windshield missing. Not a big part. In fact, it's a very small part. So small, you aren't sure if you see it correctly. The sun glares and you're a bit far away. Next thing you know, they start boarding. You panic a bit but decide to go on anyway for a closer look. You know how when you get on a plane, you can look left into the cockpit or turn right to the seats? You look left, and sure enough, part of the windshield is missing. Not a big part. Only about ten percent or so. You think somebody will notice, but the flight attendant says it's time to go. At the last second, she offers the chance for anyone to get off the plane. Are you staying on that plane? Probably not. Why aren't you staying on that plane? I mean, only ten percent of the windshield is missing. What's the big deal? The big deal is that it's a fundamental ten percent. Without it, it doesn't matter how well constructed the rest of the plane is. All of it will be destroyed without that small piece. This analogy is why many behavior plan programs and systems fail with the hardest-to-reach kids. They fail because there's almost never a component forcing adults to look in the mirror. The truth is, without being forced, we don't look, because there's nothing more uncomfortable than looking at ourselves.

Think about it. I know all of you spend a lot of hours teaching. How many of you spend a significant amount of time watching yourselves teach? It's awful. You hate how you look. You hate how you sound. You'll never need an administrator to evaluate you again because you'll pull yourself apart in ways no other human can. You'll hate everything about yourself, which is why we don't do it.

I personally believe the first line on a referral form

should ask what the adult did wrong. Second, what the adult can do differently next time. Third, what the kid did wrong, and fourth, what the kid can do differently next time. Then each person fills out the other's. Both meet and come to an agreement on what each other can do better next time.

"No, but Brian, you don't even understand. I was literally just standing by my desk and the first kid walked in and looked at the second one funny from across the room. The second one said, 'Man, what the F are you looking at?' The first one said, 'Shut the F up, B.' The second one said, 'No, you shut the F up.' Next thing you know, I'm breaking up a fight and I was literally just standing there. There's nothing I could have done differently." Maybe not, but let's examine this closer. Imagine instead of standing by your desk as kids walked in, you stood by the door. The first kid still looks at the second one funny. The second still says, "Man, what the F are you looking at?" But notice your position now. Instead of being by the desk, you're by the door, right next to the first kid. With one pivot of your left foot, you can stand between them and tell him, "Walk this way. He's trying to make you mad. If you get mad, he wins and you lose. You don't want to lose. Come on, let's walk." Then usher him out of the room.

There's a reason administrators ask us to stand by our doors when kids walk in. Explosive kids erupt quickly. Like in sports, proper position is critical. Baseball coaches constantly move fielders depending on the type of hitter. Power hitter up? Outfielders back. Super-fast leadoff batter? Infielders move in. I'm not saying everything can always be prevented. I am saying the only person I control is me.

This book focuses us internally, while most behavior plans and programs do the opposite. Notice the process for how behavior is handled in most schools. A kid misbehaves. Teacher writes a referral. Administrator delivers a consequence. Things like a time out, phone call home, detention, in-school suspension, and suspension are options. Sometimes a clip is moved from green to yellow to red. I'm not judging or criticizing those things, but notice the common denominator is each focuses on changing the kid. When that doesn't work, and we know it doesn't because the same kids are usually in trouble, we turn to things like tickets, stickers, and rewards. Again, no criticism or judgment. There's a place for them, but notice the common denominator between all focuses on changing the kid. All of it is going to crash.

If behaviors are not problems but instead solutions, it's important to understand what the problems are. The next chapter explores them in depth. The remaining chapters are a compilation of observation reports written for teachers. Much of my career is spent consulting in schools while in session. I observe classes, and meet with teachers in small groups for 30- to 45-minute blocks. I ask them to (hypothetically) bring "that one kid." Bring the one or two kids that, if we helped, would have a ripple effect on your school, class, and self. The school provides me with a note taker that takes detailed notes from each session. I send the teachers a one-page report of the most important points. My wife thought they were so good that I should put them into a book, so that's what I did.

Chapter Two
Why Kids Misbehave

There are five fundamental reasons kids misbehave and disengage in school. I've written and talked about them many times, and before getting into the consult sessions with teachers, it's important to review each as these words are the session foundations. Without understanding where the behavior comes from, it's impossible to fix.

- Attention

There are two types of "attention" kids. Let's keep it simple and call them attention A and B. "A" craves more attention because she doesn't get enough at home or anywhere else in her life. "B" gets so much at home and other places in her life, she struggles without it. Attention is the problem for both, but the solution is different. The first needs more while the second must learn to live without it. Attention is just the first reason. The kids we focus on in these sessions are usually all five at the same time.

- Power and Control

Power and control kids enjoy arguing. You know what I mean by enjoy arguing? I mean you tell them it's nice out and they say, "No it's not, it's beautiful." You're like, "Right, that's what I said." They say, "No, you said nice and it's beautiful and they're two totally different things." You say, "Well they're basically the same thing." They say, "No, because nice means this and beautiful means that." These kids will take you into a conversation and you'll look back and ask where the last ten minutes of life just went.

- Competence

Think of school like a sport. Some kids are just naturally better than others at it. What does it take to be good at the game of school? I don't know, what does it take to be good at the game of football? In football, it takes being strong, athletic, smart, and fast. In school, it takes being a good reader and writer. Be an excellent memorizer. Be great at following instructions. Some kids are just naturally better than others at the skills it takes to compete at a high level in school.

- Belonging

Like attention, there are two types of belonging kids. Belonging A is the student who struggles to belong. This kid doesn't have many friends, is socially awkward, and has a hard time fitting in. Belonging B is the student whose entire sense of belonging is tied to taking on the system. This was me as a kid. "Wait 'til Brian comes, he'll do it. Somebody get Brian, he'll say it. Brian will buy it, Brian will sell it. Go and get Brian, it's more fun when he's here." This type of kid always has to look cool in front of his friends. Tattoo those five words on your brain and don't ever forget them. From now on, every time you try figuring a kid out, start with those words. Think of a boxing ring. In the red corner are the words attention, power, control, competence and belonging. In the blue corner is the kid. Adults are the referees trying to connect the two corners. Our job is to figure out how to make that kid feel those things in this school. If we can make that kid feel those things in this school, they will no longer misbehave. How do we do it?

There is one other reason kids misbehave and disengage. I call it awareness. Some kids are literally unaware of what they're doing. An example is a student who incessantly taps their pen. You know an awareness kid because when asking them to stop, they do, and usually they're genuinely sorry. You start teaching again, and thirty seconds later they're back at it. Anytime I have awareness kids, I like to use props. For example, go down to a local carpet store and tell them you're a teacher. Ask for the plushest scraps of carpeting that they have from old jobs. Usually, they'll give them to you for free. Cut out little squares, duct tape them to the kid's desk, and say, "Do me a favor, buddy. Tap on the carpet instead of the desk because it's not really the pen tapping that's annoying, it's the noise." The goal with an awareness kid is to figure out a way for them to do their behavior without having it make me crazy, so both of us get what we need.

Chapter Three
Hear it Differently

J ackie is a fourth grader who calls out inappropriately. I counted five blurts during the half hour in the room. I remind her teacher that blurting is not the problem. It's the solution she picks to her problem. Privately, you tell her, "Jackie, I'd appreciate it if you minded your own business." As you walk away, she mumbles under her breath. Instead of continuing to walk, you turn and engage.

"Excuse me? I don't appreciate you talking to me like that," you say.

"I'll talk to you how I want," Jackie snaps.

"No you won't," you reply, upset.

"Yes I will," Jackie says.

This is a mistake many of us make. Instead, don't engage. Allow her to mumble. In chapter one, I wrote about the importance of changing *me* to change everything around me. I don't control what she says, but I control how I hear it. I pretend she mumbles this instead: "Right now, I have to call you a couple of names under my breath because if I don't, I'm going to look like a wimp in front of the entire class, and I can't look like that, so can you please be the mature adult with a college degree and continue walking away from me? I have to eat lunch with them, and I have to ride the bus with them, and I have to be around them all day long. After all, what do you tell us to do when someone calls us a name? You tell us to just turn and walk away. How come you can't? After all, Mr. Mendler, what do you tell us to do when someone says something that we don't like? You tell us to just ignore it. How come you can't? If you did, I would really appreciate it. Thank you very much, sir."

Imagine a student mumbling that. Would you go marching back? I will argue that's exactly what the student is saying in the only way they can say it. They can't say it any other way, so she calls me a name or two under her breath. Her teacher is concerned about how it will look to other students if she lets Jackie mumble. Will they believe it's okay to call her names then, too? This is a valid concern. Eliminate this by using a prevention technique. Tell students what will happen before it does:

"Unfortunately, meaning I wish this wasn't going to happen, but I know it will, some of you might do and say some rude, nasty, inappropriate, not nice, mean things this year. I just want to let you know that I hope it doesn't, but if and when it does, I will not always stop my lessons to deal with it. It doesn't mean I didn't hear it, because probably I did, and it doesn't mean I'm not going to do anything about it, probably I will. However, in the moment something happens in our class, sometimes it might look like I'm ignoring behavior. That's how it might look to some of you. Trust me, I'm not ignoring it. Sometimes I think teaching those of you who behave appropriately is more important at that moment than stopping for one or two who are behaving inappropriately. For example, I might drop by your desk, table, or area and say, 'Knock it off, cut it out, or enough is enough.' As I walk away, someone might mumble inappropriate things about me. Their best friend might say, 'Oh Mr. Mendler! Did you hear that? You're just gonna let her say that to you?' Yes, I heard it, and yes, I will deal with it. It just might not be at the moment you think I should. Any consequence I choose to give or not to give will be between that student and me, and their parents, and nobody else. I will not share everyone's business with the entire class. Sound good?"

Now the teacher has ultimate control and can choose to stop and engage or continue walking away without worrying about what everyone thinks. I am constantly reminding my students of this throughout the year.

Jackie is desperate for attention. Sometimes she sticks up for the teacher, telling other students to be quiet or do their work. The teacher doesn't like it because she thinks her control is diminished. I ask how specifically she handles it when Jackie does this. The teacher reminds Jackie her job is to be a student. Then she moves on.

My suggestion is to pull Jackie aside and privately compliment her. "I love when people are assertive, and I appreciate you sticking up for me. It means a lot. At the same time, do you see how it might look like I don't have control if you fight my battles? What do you think about allowing me to correct them next time? If I'm unsuccessful, you can have a try. But I really do appreciate you sticking up for me." Notice how I compliment her strengths and thank her for helping me? Then I follow up with questions. For kids who like arguing, statements are fuel and questions are kryptonite.

Instead of, "We don't talk to adults like that," which started the whole back and forth, get on her level and privately (with or without eye contact) say, "I'm just curious. Can you please tell me where you learned to talk to adults that way? Does someone talk to you that way that makes you think that's an okay way to talk to me? Would you like to tell me? Because I know that's not you talking in there. Who is talking in there?" Questions disarm the kid because they can't be argued. I recommend picking one day of your life, and from the minute you wake up in the morning until the minute you go to bed at night, no matter what anyone does, no matter what anyone says, you're only allowed to use questions, and see what happens.

A student asks, "Mr. Mendler, what's the homework going to be?"

I reply with, "I don't know, what do y'all think it should be? You think twenty problems or fifteen? Or how about I give you twenty and you pick whichever ten you want?"

They ask, "Mr. Mendler, what's the consequence going to be if I break that rule?"

I say, "Oh my gosh, I'm not really sure. What's it going to take for you to stop calling people names? We both know the first ten things I've tried this year haven't worked. Do you have any ideas for me?"

Power struggles are like landmines and must be avoided at all costs. Stepping on one can blow off your foot.

Jackie often gets in trouble by retaliating against a boy who "makes her mad." The goal is for her to focus on what she can control. Explain how and why retaliating hurts her more than the other person. Teach her that every time she gets mad, he wins and she loses. Talk about mental toughness. In sports, there are people who try to distract you all the time. Stay focused on what you are there to accomplish. Talk about having the ability to stay calm when things around you get crazy.

"Down one point on the road, no time on the clock. You go to the hoop hard and get fouled. On the line, do you think the crowd is going to be nice and calm or do you think they'll be trying to distract you in every way possible? This is practice for that. Anytime he makes you mad, pretend you're on the line. He's trying to make you miss. Can you remain focused and nail the shot anyway?" Talk about remaining respectful to disrespectful people and what an amazing character trait that is. Use the word "power." In general, people don't like feeling like they give up their own power.

"Can you see how it seems like he takes away your power? Why give up your power so easily? In your mind, you stick up for yourself, but I see it as you giving him a lot of power." I'm not saying not to deal with the person making her mad. I'm saying she has no control over what that person does or says. Control yourself, and you will control everything around you—that advice isn't just for adults.

The teacher asks about her learning lab that is twenty minutes long. They don't listen and are not quiet. She's not able to teach. I ask if she is not able to teach, or if she's not able to teach what she planned, because those are very different things. In education, there are two things that live at the same time. There's "What I'm supposed to teach," which comes from basically everyone but the teacher. It comes from administrators, board members, people at the state, etc... I honestly don't know where it comes from. What I do know is, it's real and causes lots of stress.

Then there's this other thing living at the same time called, "What kids need to learn." Let me be clear; I don't ever think teaching is easy, but it's easiest when what I'm supposed to teach is also what kids need to learn. The problem right now is they're on opposite coasts. What I'm supposed to teach is in New York and what they need to learn is in Los Angeles, and teachers are getting caught in Iowa, torn between the two. I'm supposed to teach three plus three, but they need to learn how to say please and thank you. I'm supposed to teach Shakespeare, but they have no idea how to respectfully disagree with each other. *Supposed to* versus *need to* is the exhaustion and burnout engulfing our profession right now.

Any time I feel this pull, I go hard teaching what they need, and trust that doing so is the path back to where I'm supposed to be. I recently flew from Tampa, connecting in Detroit, to Omaha. It doesn't make sense, but it was the best route for me that day. Remember, lesson plans are just plans and sometimes plans change. An example of this follows in the next chapter.

Chapter Four
Stay Awake

Today I worked at a charter school outside Pittsburgh. The first student we discussed was a fifth grade boy who constantly falls asleep. I don't just mean closing eyes for a snooze. I'm talking out cold with drool. The teachers are very frustrated. Always look at the bright side first. At least he sleeps and doesn't destroy the room. Usually sleepers don't ruin other people's learning. In every situation, there is something to be grateful for.

I ask if there is anything that keeps him awake. They tell me he loves watching YouTube videos. If he can watch videos for the whole class, he stays awake but still gets nothing done. I ask what videos he loves watching. Two of the three teachers in our group shake their heads and roll their eyes. Almost insulted by my question, they have no idea. The third says, "I know. He loves anything related to animation and animals." I ask her to be more specific and to tell me about some of the videos he watches. She doesn't know. This is the first task. Dive head first into his world. Right now the teachers are on their own island with their content and lessons. The kid is on his island with videos that he loves. The teachers want him to come to their island and learn the lesson that they planned. *Come over to my world.*

The problem is the kid isn't interested in coming because they're growing up in a delivery world. In a world where if you have a product and you don't bring it to my doorstep, I don't want it. Amazon started the whole thing. They made it so I never again have to step foot in Target or Wal-Mart because with one swipe on my phone, the toothpaste shows up at my door, usually cheaper and faster. It used to be that I had to order a pizza or Chinese food if I didn't feel like making dinner and didn't want to go out. Now, I open Uber Eats or Grubhub, and where I live, 168 different restaurants will bring food to my door.

We live in a world of Snapchat and Instagram. A world of instant bring-it-to-me-immediately-right-now-or-I-don't-want-it. Think about the measures society took for Covid. They wouldn't even have been possible just a few years ago. There was no Zoom to deliver content to our kitchen tables, or Instacart to drop groceries at our front doors. Almost every aspect of life has a delivery component now. When I listen to music or a podcast, it has to come with me wherever I go. If I can't seamlessly transfer from TV to phone to headphones to the car and back, I'm not interested. This is the world these kids have created.

I used to have to drive a half hour to and from my recovery meetings, sometimes in snowy weather, all the while thinking about the dishes needing to be done or bedtime routines I was missing. When traveling out of state, I had to miss the meeting completely. Now I log onto Zoom and join a meeting from wherever I am at that moment. I turn off my camera, put on my headphones, and do the dishes while listening to the meeting in my house. This year alone I've attended virtual recovery meetings from seven different airports. The meeting comes to me, wherever I am. I don't have to go to it anymore.

My point is the stuff they create (their world) is usually better anyway. Instead of trying to get him to come over, dive into the water and swim over to his island. Immerse yourself in the videos with him. Why are they so fascinating? What does he love about them so much? During the process, keep an eye glanced back at your island (the content). What do I have over there I can bring with me to his island? I'm not going back to my island. The party is over here now, but I still have my stuff back there, and lots of that stuff is interesting. Plus, I have to teach it. When nobody is looking, go back and pick one or two things to bring over. He loves YouTube. I'm teaching basic fractions. How do I connect basic fractions to YouTube? Explain about the paid partnership program where content creators earn money based on how many clicks they receive on a video. Research what makes a great video. How is a thumbnail created? Every video has a caption usually with at least one adjective. There is also a description on every video (ELA).

According to Forbes, YouTube's biggest star, MrBeast, made $54 million in 2021, double the amount that he'd earned the previous year. Most of his money comes from ad revenue generated by the 90+ million subscribers who tune into his channel (looper.com). The kid loves YouTube. I'm guessing he loves money too. Show him the connection.

Remember, power struggles are to be avoided at all costs. This means even if I don't like him sleeping, sometimes it's better than arguing with him. When awake, I'm diving head first into his world, all the while trying to connect what I have (my lesson plan) to what he already enjoys. During my interactions with him in his world, I can now start to really understand his sleeping.

As we are watching a video or talking about a description, I can ask, "Hey man, you know I look bad when you fall asleep in my class, right? Is there anything I can do to help keep you awake? If my admin comes in and sees you sleeping or other kids see you sleeping, I'm going to catch some heat. What's going on with you? Want to tell me?" This conversation happens on his island. Once he trusts me, believes in me, and realizes I care more about him than about anything I'm trying to teach him, I'll be able to teach him anything I want. Finally, stay focused on what you control. You don't control what he does or says, but you always control how you respond to what he does and says. That's your focus every day, along with all other suggestions.

Chapter Five

The Number One Relationship-Building Rule

Cole is set off any time a teacher expects him to do something he doesn't like. Teachers were often born last-word type people. Meaning in conversations, we frequently need to be the last person who says something. Focus on becoming a second-to-last-word person instead. Say what you need to say and move on. Think of it like a hit and run. "I believe I saw you drop that piece of paper and I'd appreciate it if you picked it up, thanks." Then get out of there. Walk away. Don't stick around for the argument. Focus on using questions instead of statements. Instead of, "You need to take off those headphones," say, "I love your headphones and I wear them myself frequently. I'm not at all against you wearing them, but right now I'm curious, what exactly do you need them for? Is there any chance you can give me fifteen solid minutes of work with them off? How long do you plan on using them? If you choose not to take them off at the agreed upon time, what should happen?" Oppositional kids argue because they can. Questions can't be argued.

The teacher admits she hasn't spent much time consciously building a relationship with Cole. One of my relationship-building rules is that required time doesn't count. Required time is time an administrator puts a kid on my schedule. If I don't count this time, how much extra time do I spend on a daily basis getting to know him or her? Her answer (like most when I ask this question) is none. I recommend starting with two minutes every day. I prefer asking a colleague if I can borrow him from their class for a couple of minutes during my free time. I've never had one say no. In fact, usually they ask why only two minutes. I start the conversation by saying to the kid, "Just so you know, this is my free time. Meaning I could be anywhere in the school right now doing whatever I want and I'm choosing to spend this time with you. This is how bad of a job I've done this year getting to know you. I think I've done a good job teaching you math (or science or social studies) but a bad job of understanding who you are. That ends today." Then I tell the student we're going to walk around the school for two minutes and that I've set some ground rules for our conversation. The rules are not in stone and can be changed if the student disagrees with any of them. "Rule number one is you are allowed to ask me anything you want to know about me. Anything in the whole world. Rule number two is I'm allowed to ask you anything I want to know about you. Anything in the whole world. Rule number three is that neither of us are required to answer. Meaning if you don't feel comfortable answering, just say, 'Mr. Mendler, I don't feel comfortable answering that.' I'll do the same. There are certain things that, by law, I am required to report. Please keep that in mind. I also recommend steering really far away from anything related to religion, politics, gender, and sex." If any of those topics come up, I refer the student to the counselor, psychologist, or social worker.

Rule number four is neither of us are allowed to get mad at the other person for asking. Sometimes I ask questions just trying to know someone that inadvertently strikes a nerve. For example, once I asked a student what she was doing over Christmas break, and I got yelled at. "Don't ask me what I am doing over break. It's none of your f'ing business," is exactly what she said. I try to make it clear that my intention is never to make a student upset, and if I do, to give my apologies.

Rule number five only applies to me. I promise not to talk about school. Kids can talk about whatever they want, but I won't bring up school. I also tell the students that I'll never hide something from their parents or guardians and it's my intention to get to know them better as well. Then we start, and the things I get to know about kids (and vice versa) are invaluable. Some people ask what two minutes are really going to do? It's not very much time. I agree, but it's not about the two minutes today. It's about two minutes today multiplied by five days in a week. That's ten minutes per week, multiplied by four weeks in a month, multiplied by ten months in a school year. That's 400 minutes a year of one-on-one time with Cole. Two minutes is too much? Fine, one minute per day still equals 200 minutes a year. The pushback from some teachers is they don't have enough time. Strangely those same people often spend that amount of time (or more) writing referrals. See it as an investment. I have three kids, two dogs and a wife. Literally every dollar I earn working could immediately go back out. I still put a little bit away every month because people who know better say if I continue to do this consistently, month after month, a few years from now I will be blown away by how much I have. Same concept here. If he refuses to answer questions during the walk, simply answer your own question. Tell him about your favorite food, sports teams, vacation spots, etc. Relationships are a two-way street. I learn about you, and you learn about me. Sometimes we want kids to give up all sorts of information, but we don't want to give much back. How would your relationship work at home if you learned all about your spouse, but they got nothing in return? Probably not great.

Finally, the teacher tells me that Cole loves talking about technology. He constantly takes things apart and puts them back together. Utilize this by finding broken electronics or devices and allow him to work on them. Show him how he can buy something, fix it, and resell it for more money. List the items on Ebay. Allow him to write the description (ELA) and figure out shipping costs (math). Teach him how amazing it is that he enjoys this. Maybe he can start a YouTube channel teaching people how to refurbish electronics. Again, notice I'm diving into his world.

I'm told that Cole is usually pretty well behaved in the morning. He's also good when he has a class job (power and control). He recently lost iPad privileges for intentionally smashing a keyboard. The teacher is deciding when to give it back. I recommend bringing him into the process. Again, you want him to feel like he is making the decisions you would make for him anyway. Say, "How long will it take for you to remember that breaking things on purpose is unacceptable?" Be willing to negotiate with him. During the week, praise him for making a decision and let him know he is doing well. You might even give it back to him early if he thinks he earned it. If I were his teacher, there would always be some type of project related to taking apart and fixing technology. This skill alone will make him very successful in life, the ultimate goal of any teacher.

We also discuss the social aspect of other kids knowing he's in the special education room. Today he said, "I'm really mad at my mom for putting me in here."

The teacher responds, "Well, it's too bad. There's nothing I can do about it." Instead, try saying, "I understand you feel upset, and I'd probably be mad too." Then try to relate. "When I was in sixth grade, my parents pulled me out of school completely. My academic skills were super low, and my behavior was out of control. They sent me to tour a new school for a day. When I came home, they asked how I liked it. I told them it was fine, but I was really glad I didn't have to go there. They told me I was starting full time the next day. I was furious. I didn't get to say goodbye to my friends or anything. So I promise, I get it, and I'm really sorry you have to be in a place you don't want to be. If there's anything I can do to make it better, please let me know. I was not the one who put you here, but I can teach you how to get out if that interests you. Acting inappropriately when you get the opportunity to go into other rooms doesn't help, I promise. It makes other teachers think this is the right place for you. I'll advocate for you to move out of this room, but only if I can count on you not to make either one of us look bad. What do you think?"

I realize that what happened to you may not have exactly happened to your student, but we all have a story in our lives about being in an uncomfortable or frustrating situation and pushing through. Share your story. The goal is to ease his anxiety and build a relationship at the same time.

Cole's mom rarely follows through. He has no biological dad, but has a stepdad who can't stand him. It's important to remember that all of us frequently take out our biggest annoyances, aggravations, and frustrations in our lives on people we actually love and care about most. From this perspective, it makes sense he "unloads" his baggage in this room. He wants you to give up on him because that's what he expects. Be tougher in not quitting than he is in trying to get you to. View him as a challenge to overcome and try hard to

see the small gains made. It's easy to focus on the negative.
Sometimes we need to take a step back and really look for the
good. Never hold grudges. They usually hurt the holder more
than the person we are holding against.

Chapter Six
Connection is Key

Today I'm in a ninth grade math class. Jameson is a name I hear from many teachers throughout the day. He has a hard time focusing for longer periods of time. Just because the school says a period is 45 or 90 minutes, doesn't mean a student can focus that long. Break the time into multiple mini lessons. Show the written agenda. I primarily taught ELA, so here is an example from my class:

9-9:20 a.m. – Read and discuss two poems / figurative language
9:20-9:40 a.m. – Read out loud chapter 6 of Mice and Men
9:40-10 a.m. – Discuss / answer questions from reading
10-10:20 a.m. – Free writing / catch up on missed work

The class is mostly quiet, waiting for the teacher to begin her lesson. A couple of girls in the back whisper. The teacher looks at them and says, "I'll wait." If I was in that class, you'd be waiting all year. My entire goal was to keep you waiting. Instead of waiting, teach hard from the start. Of course, slow down for questions or if someone doesn't understand something, but waiting for everyone to be perfectly quiet is a recipe for disaster.

It depends on the day with Jameson. Yesterday was mostly good. He kicked a desk on his way in, but other than that remained on task. He even helped other students. I remind the teacher to intensely (and privately) praise him for doing the right things. Get in his ear and say, "I love how you help others. I'm proud of you." Then walk away. Don't stick around for a response.

We often correct kids intensely. "Knock it off! Cut it out! Enough is enough! Stop already!" Jameson has learned that acting inappropriately gains attention. The goal is to flip this. Privately praise with the same (if not more) intensity. The goal is for him to learn that the way to gain attention is by doing the right thing. As always, connection is also key. Focus on basic skills. Give him leadership roles. Tell him how much you believe in him. Make it very clear that behaviors are not the problem, but the solution to his problems. Show him how similar the two of you are. I have to be a teammate before I can be a coach. He needs to know I want to win as badly as he does.

Say to him, "It's kind of scary how similar we are. You get annoyed, sometimes as do I. I often say things and the second they come out, I want to put them back in. Ever happen to you? See how similar we are? The only difference between us (and it is a slight one) is when I get angry, annoyed, or frustrated, I don't kick desks. Sometimes I feel like kicking them, but I don't. One rule I learned in addiction recovery is, 'if it feels amazing in the short term, it's usually really bad for me in the long term.' Vice versa is also true. When something hurts a lot in the short term, it's almost always really good for me in the long term. I admit kicking feels good sometimes, but think about what happens next. You get in trouble, your parents get called, you get suspended, you get grounded, you miss more school, and you get farther behind. Why do you want to hurt yourself?"

Jameson says, "Well, I don't."

I reply with, "Great. Do you have any interest in learning some strategies to handle your anger?"

I love to exercise. I don't care where I am or who is around. Any time I feel like biting, kicking, punching, hitting, or spitting, I exercise instead. I recently did fifty push-ups in the Denver airport after United Airlines canceled a flight at midnight after delaying us for three hours. I wanted to lose it. Instead, I dropped and did push-ups until I couldn't do them anymore. Then I sat up and calmly figured out how to get where I needed to go. Doing as many push-ups, sit-ups, and squats as possible changes my focus.

Next, I focus on my breathing. Tiring out from exercising raises the heart rate. Take long, drawn-out, slow breaths counting backwards from thirty. Then I make a list of what went wrong and how I can fix it. All of this must be discussed and practiced during times of calm. Once in a while, challenge a student to do ten push-ups, squats, or burpees when things are going well, just to get them used to doing them regularly.

This class is learning "point of origin," sitting at their desks with the teacher writing on the board. She talks at them with no examples. Maybe use sports?

Where does a game start? The point of origin: 0-0.
Origin = original or origination. The game originates
(starts) at points 0-0.

Pay attention to how many times you say "for
example" in a day. The more the better. My wife was a
high school math teacher for ten years. One of her
favorite activities was taking students on a field trip
around the school. She used lines on the basketball
court to teach angles, X & Y axis, etc. Students start at a
point of origin (place where two lines meet) and
physically plot points with their bodies (over three, up
five). This shows that angles are literally everywhere.
Look at ceiling corners for 90-degree angles. Floor
curves and stairwells are great for teaching angles as
well. Again, go to their world. What do they love?
What are their interests? If they have one hour at
home to do whatever they want, what is it? When I'm
not exactly sure, I will either ask the student or offer
one of seven categories: sports, music, video games,
money, animals, art, and movies. Most kids enjoy at
least one. Focus on connecting what they enjoy to
origin, fractions, percentages, etc.

I told her of a former student, Tara, who
constantly made little comments and jokes with two
other girls she sat near. I couldn't get her to stop. Out
of frustration and anger I said, "I don't know what to do
with you anymore. If you were me, what would you
do?"

In a very calm voice she said, "I would just move
my seat."

I said, "What?"

She said, "I would just move my seat. The
problem is I don't have any friends."

I said, "What do you mean?"

She replied, "How many meanings does that have? I don't have any friends. I don't even really like the girls I sit near, and I definitely don't want to act like them. I also don't think they're funny. I kinda feel like I have to laugh at them and act like they're funny because when we leave here, they sit by me at lunch. They talk to me. They want to be around me. But Mr. Mendler, please don't move my seat like most teachers do."

I had no idea what she meant, but luckily, my paraprofessional did. The rule is at least three for one. If I have to move a seat, I move three instead. This eliminates, "You always pick on me, you never pick on anyone else." I actually left Tara alone and moved the other two. Sometimes students give us great ideas. I'm not going to say she was perfect, but her behavior definitely improved. My para said, "Maybe you want to ask their opinion more often."

By the way, anytime a student says, "You always pick on me and never anyone else," try hard not to get defensive. Instead say, "Oh my gosh, I'm so sorry. I never mean to pick on anyone. Can you please give me some examples of how I pick on you?" I once had a student who said this to me, and when she explained, it actually made sense. Of course, I saw it as I was pushing her because she was a kid with a ton of potential.

Chapter Seven
Disruptive and Out of Control

The teacher enters our meeting annoyed and frustrated. I ask why and she says, "Administration here doesn't support us. I've sent Darryl to the office like a million times this year and they always just send him back. He's out of control and I'm disgusted by the lack of support."

I ask, "What would you like them to do?"

"Something. I mean, there's just no support," she replied.

"I hear you, and I'm not disagreeing or saying you're wrong. I am curious what you would like them to do." I said.

"Well, I don't really know. All I know is these kids show no respect to anyone..." she said.

I struggle when educators complain about not feeling supported. Of course, the goal is to give teachers the best chance at success. On the other hand, complaining about something that is subjective is frustrating to administrators. Support means different things to different people, and to say "I don't feel it" without giving specific examples of what I need the giver to do makes me sound like a whiner.

It's a bit hypocritical to kick a kid out "a million times" while simultaneously complaining someone else isn't doing a good enough job. Sort of like batting leadoff in a baseball game and striking out. Then complaining about your teammate striking out next. Instead, focus on what you can control. What kind of relationship have you built with him? Have you spent extra one-on-one time with him outside of class? What kind of classroom jobs does he have? Is there a way for him to help someone else? Each time we remove a student from class, another layer of our own power is stripped away. The message sent is, "I can't handle you myself, and I need help." Sort of like the mom (or dad) who says, "You wait until Daddy (or Mommy) comes home. They'll deal with this." The best mommies (or daddies) say, "I don't care if Daddy (or Mommy) ever comes home. Get back in bed now," and they aren't playing. Again, I'm not saying never to remove a kid, but it should be difficult.

I learned from an administrator that there are only two scenarios where it is okay to "throw away one person's education to save twenty others'."

- Physical violence (kid on kid or kid on adult)
- Things are literally so bad I can't teach

Everything else should be handled in the classroom. Use discretion when enforcing rules. Some teachers think they need to enforce everything all the time. This is ridiculous. If every person who didn't come to a complete stop at every stop sign got pulled over, we would have chaos in our society. I'm not saying not to enforce rules. I'm saying if the rule says "no gum chewing" and the kid is quietly chewing a piece of gum in the corner at his desk, I'm not picking a potential argument by telling him to spit it out. I might privately say to him, "You know we aren't supposed to have gum in here right? You know if my boss sees it, I'm going to get in trouble. I prefer not to have that happen so please don't let me hear or see it again. If I do, I might have to ask you to spit it out. Cool?" Then walk away.

I prefer expectations to rules. The former indicates what to do, while the latter indicates what not to do. No hitting (rule) versus keep hands and feet to yourselves (expectation). Both should be specific and measurable, otherwise it's easy for kids to get confused. In this classroom the rule says, "be respectful." Another says, "be responsible." Respect and responsibility are not rules or expectations because they're subjective words. They mean different things to different people, thus can't be measured. They're more important than rules. I call them values.

In my room, we have expectations and values. The values answer why a student should do something. The expectations answer specifically what a student should do. Values are broad and often can't be measured. Responsibility is a value. Based on the value of responsibility, we will bring a notebook and pencil to class every day.

"Where is your notebook?" I ask a student.

"Well I was just—" they begin to say.

"You were just what? Where is your notebook?" I say.

"But we were just—" the student tries to say again.

"Where is your notebook? Either you have it or you don't."

"Why does it matter if I bring a notebook every day? Seriously, you have like twenty notebooks, can't I just borrow one? You're kind of crazy about this, Mr. Mendler."

I say, "Good point, and you're right. I do have like twenty notebooks. The truth is, I don't care at all about the notebook. I care that you become a responsible person. I worry that someday you play on my varsity baseball team and twenty minutes to an away game, I hear from the back of the bus, 'Oh shoot, coach, I forgot my cleats.' Or, 'Dang, coach, I didn't know we were wearing red jerseys. I brought white.' The goal isn't for you to bring your notebook every day. The goal is for you to become a responsible person."

Anytime a student complains about following a rule or expectation, explain it by talking about a value. This is how to know when we have a bad or outdated rule or expectation. Answers like "because I said so" or "because that's the way it's always been" or, my favorite, "because it's in our handbook" let me know I need to revisit the expectation and possibly change it.

I ask about Darryl's home life. The teacher says, "I know it's not good. I'm not one hundred percent sure, but I think he has a few brothers and sisters and I know, well I am not sure, but I think there is a mom. Wait, maybe it's his grandma."

When we really know a kid, the answer should sound like this: "He has three brothers and two sisters. His mother is super nice but completely overwhelmed. She tries hard but works two jobs, so supervision is minimal at home. His older siblings are not interested in helping much. Three years ago, their father walked out on the family. Just picked up and left. Didn't tell anyone where he was going. This devastated Darryl and now he doesn't trust adults. Especially adult men. Deep down he thinks everyone is going to abandon him, so he's built walls around him. It's easier not to get close than to get close and have the closeness ripped away. Last year, he tried out for basketball and didn't make it. This was upsetting not because of basketball but because he needed something to belong to." Relationships with hard-to-reach kids are valuable. Creating valuable things takes time, patience, energy, and effort. Valuable things can also be ruined in seconds. I was in New York on September 11, 2001. They knocked the twin towers down in one morning. It took almost twenty years to rebuild. Relationship-building is a marathon, not a sprint. Stay with it. Pace yourself. Chip away every day.

Chapter Eight
Behavior Whack-A-Mole

I am asked what to do when an entire group is challenging. The first step is to narrow it down to one or two. If X is absent, I can get everyone else to behave. If not just X, then how many? Make a list of names with the mission to connect with them one at a time. Leadership will emerge, so if you're not sure, take a day and simply observe. This is true for all age groups. Lord of the Flies. Put a bunch of kids on an island with no adult supervision and watch how they act. Who runs the show? Who do they pay attention and listen to? Observe after school, before school, during free periods, during lunch.

My goal is to build relationships so tight with the leaders, they will want to work for instead of against me. Focus on changing one or two. *I need them more than they need me* is my mentality. They control others. Remember, required time does not count for connection with these kids. How much extra time do I spend connecting? Be sure if the extra time is done one-on-one, it is in a public place with at least one other adult close by. Think two minutes a day for ten straight days.

I am the head coach of the classroom. I am in charge, but good head coaches have assistants and captains. Fill those roles with these kids. Ask for their opinions. Make them group leaders. Is there a younger student (from a different grade) they can be paired with? Almost like an in-school big brother, big sister program. Help them with issues in other teachers' classes. The process will take time. Be patient. Focus on prevention with the leaders.

First thing in the morning, privately ask, "Hey, what's going on with you? How are things going to be today? What can I expect? Can I count on you to behave? How many minutes of good behavior do you think I will see? Can you keep track or should I?" Notice my questions are firm, direct, and short. Is this going to be a good or bad day, a good morning or a bad morning, a good ten minutes or a bad ten minutes? Usually, the younger the age, the more frequently I check in. Learn to embrace the journey. Remember that changing behaviors is a roller coaster ride filled with ups, downs, loops, corkscrews, and tunnels with hidden dips. This is true for all of us.

Think of something you've tried to change about yourself. Were you perfect at it from the start or did you have good days and bad days? Sometimes even a good hour is followed by a bad one. During the down cycle of the ride (which we all have), from the people closest to you, what do you need from them every single time? Whatever your answer, kids need the same.

Most reward systems fail when they require good behavior all day or all week. I remember in fourth grade, if we behaved all week, we attended Fun Friday. I often lost this privilege by 10 a.m. on Monday morning. That's four and a half days to figure out who to take down with me. You better believe I'm not going to be the only one left out of Fun Friday. Be very careful with definitive policies. Use words like usually, frequently, most of the time, and often when creating them. "Usually if a student does not behave all week, they will not attend Fun Friday. However, I always reserve the right to change my mind and all final decisions will be made one minute before Fun Friday begins." Instead of bringing people down with me, now there is incentive for my classmate to say, "No, Bri, shut up for a day. Maybe she'll forget. Remember she doesn't actually decide until right before it starts. So be good for a day or two."

Sometimes we create policies that get in our own way. I remember working in a school where there was an automatic, no questions asked, five-day suspension for fighting. This might sound good on the surface, but what if a kid tried to walk away and ended up fighting back in self-defense? Should that kid really get the same consequence or punishment as the kid who started it? The policy should say, "Most of the time, when kids fight, they will get a five-day suspension. However, all final decisions will be made by people, not by pieces of paper." Now we can use our policy and our brain. Again, the goal is to give ourselves the advantage. I always want to be fluid in my ability to make decisions. Strict policies often get in the way with the hardest-to-reach kids.

A classic symptom of oppositional defiance is the constant need to feel power and control. Generally at home, these kids think they are in charge. With many oppositional kids, there is not much structure at home. They stay up until all hours and play video games without much supervision. Oftentimes, it's a single-parent family struggling to follow through. Mom says to be in for dinner at 5 p.m., and the kid walks in at 6:30 p.m. instead. Not only is there no consequence, but Mom says, "Here's your dinner, honey, and when you're finished, I will clean it up for you too because I just love you so much."

I call this child abuse. Not the kind we call Child Protective Services for, nor should it be, because they have enough to do with the other kind of abuse. But now, this kid comes to school and doesn't take the expectations seriously. For example, we may ask students to wait in line. He thinks, *wait in line? I don't wait in line at home. Eat when you tell me it's lunchtime? At home I eat what I want, when I want, where I want. Sometimes I even sit on the floor, and when finished, I walk away and magically it gets cleaned up for me. Raise my hand? Share?* This student has never learned how to do these things.

I often hear teachers say the words "I need" a lot. "I need you to sit down. I need you to line up. Y'all, I need you to take out your books." As a kid, I didn't care what the teacher needed. Who talks to people like that, anyway? Sometimes adults talk to kids in ways they would never talk to any other person in their life. I can only imagine coming home from a work trip and saying to my wife, "I need you to do my laundry," or, "I need you to cook my dinner." I would get slapped up one side and down the other, and rightfully so. Replace "I need" with any of the following:

"Thank you for…"
"I would appreciate it if…"
"What do you think about?"
"Do you mind?"
"It would be great to see…"

Basically anything is better than "I need."

Chapter Nine
Group Work Advice / Sarcasm

observe Nicco, a second grade boy outside Jacksonville, Florida. He shouts a few times in class, obviously seeking attention. My immediate thought is to agree with him on a predetermined number of shouts, or let him choose the number and then monitor it. The goal is for him to track his own behavior. Remember, shouting isn't his problem, it's the solution he has chosen to his problems (attention, power, control, competence, belonging). He is probably all five at the same time. If a student runs at full speed, they must slow down before stopping. We often want immediate changes, but Nicco, and kids like him, didn't become this way overnight.

We don't change them overnight. Remember, valuable things take time. The goal is to reduce the number of outbursts while simultaneously getting him to think about his behavior. This is true when calling on him as well. Say, "Okay, Nicco, your one minute," (or however long you agree upon), "starts now." Of course if he's in the middle of a sentence and time runs out, he gets to finish. Specific start and end times are important, otherwise some kids will ramble.

Focus on his need for attention. Privately praise him for doing the boring, mundane things he's supposed to do anyway. "I love how you just pushed in your chair. Great job." Since you have him all day, these conversations can happen in class or during extra time spent with him (outside of required time). Always be on the lookout for ways he can help others.

You tell me transitions are really hard for him, so be sure to plan for them. Forty-five minutes before moving to music class, tell him, "You know you have music today, and that lady is strict. She doesn't like when kids talk during class. Is it possible for you to remain quiet the whole time? If you get angry, what can you do instead of calling her names? I'm counting on you to give me a detailed report after class of how it went, are you good with this? Can I trust you?"

This type of conversation happens during times of calm before each transition. Again, before any transition, privately check in and say, "You know we're going from our desk to the carpet in ten minutes, right? Can I count on you to go without touching other people's things? Do you think you can quietly help me get everyone seated in the right place? If this one or that one sits next to you, is everything going to be okay? Can you handle yourself or might I have to move you? What do you think? I'm going to read a book. Should it be this one or that one? Which one do you think your friends will like more? Want to take the next ten minutes to flip through both and decide which is better?" These are some examples of questions you might ask your student. Questions avoid arguments and allow kids to make decisions. Use them often.

You ask for some tips to make group work better. I prefer no more than five members in a group. Six or more is usually a problem because there isn't enough for everyone to do. Number each member of the group one to five. Then give each a specific task. Numbers one and five stay the same no matter what content or grade I teach. Two, three, and four change based on the activity. Role number one is the group leader. This is most important.

I'm the general manager of this classroom. I watch from the press box. My name is on the door. Everything that happens starts and stops with me. Leaders are managers on the field, making sure everyone else on the team successfully does their job. Number two reads. Three takes notes. Four organizes the notes. Five speaks and presents information. Five can't do her job without four doing hers. Four can't do her job without three doing his, and so on. Number one manages the whole thing.

Categories vary based on activity needs. I don't always change up roles if things are working. The Yankees don't put their starting shortstop at catcher just to change it up. For the most part, position students where they're best. Some are natural leaders. Others are better at reading. The only required rotating role is presenter because public speaking is rarely required in school. If I have a student that doesn't want to present or is super shy, I'll pair them with a strong leader. Then I'll privately say to the leader, "You see who is in your group? He doesn't love talking in front of people. Make sure you stand right next to him. You can even jump in if need be. You are not going to let him fail. I'm watching your leadership skills as much as his presenting skills during this, understood?" Because it's easier to extend something to a kid than take something away from them, figure out how much time an activity will take and then cut it in half. If I believe an activity will take thirty minutes, I tell students they have fifteen. This creates more urgency. If students are working well after fifteen minutes, I can extend and no one even notices. By contrast, try taking time away, and inevitably someone complains. Next, I gather the leaders around me like I'm coaching a basketball team. I remind them of some basic leadership skills, and each is given a red, yellow, and green plastic drinking cup. Red tells me (without asking) to stop because the group needs significant help. Yellow means they have a quick question and I just have to slow down. They might want to ask, "How much time do we have again?" or, "How do you pronounce this word?" Green means keep moving and that all is good. Now I can allow them to work without being the annoying teacher constantly asking if everyone is doing okay. It also gives the teacher a few minutes of chill time if they see green all around. Sometimes I'll put all of my strugglers in the same group knowing they'll be red, and all other groups will be green. Now I can give them extra help, without worrying if the others need me during that time.

Explain that during group time, there are only six people allowed to talk to the teacher. "If you are not a group leader, please do not come to me. I don't want to hear from you. Go to your leader. They will help or come to me." Now instead of managing thirty students, we only have to pay attention to six. Like captains on a football or soccer team who take charge on the field, group leaders allow us to manage a large group while focusing on only a few. Referees will only talk to the captains. If you're not a captain they don't want to hear from you. Focus on chain of command and leadership skills.

Finally, I'm asked if it's okay to be sarcastic with kids. Many educators recommend never being sarcastic. I personally don't like the words always and never. To me, sarcasm is like an extremely dangerous chemical in the chemistry lab. If you don't know how to use it, stay away, because it can blow up the relationship with a student. But when used properly, it can be a relationship-building tool. Sometimes kids don't get when you're being sarcastic with them. If that happens, apologize quickly and passionately.

Say, "I'm so sorry. Sometimes I joke around with people. I was totally messing with you. I made a mistake. It won't happen again." Also, if I'm able to dish it, I'd better be able to take it. I once worked with a teacher that was frequently sarcastic with kids. When they gave it back, she wrote them up. Either we dish it and take it, or we do neither.

A student got me good one time. You know they get you good when you get mad for real. One of my high school seniors had a brand new, bright yellow polo shirt on. The shirt looked really good on him. I said, "That's a great shirt. I love it. It looks really good on you. Of course you know it would be better on me, right?"

He said, "Yeah, good one, Mr. Mendler. You know what I do have that would look fantastic on you for real?"

"What?" I asked.

He said, "Hair. You'd love some, wouldn't you?" The class erupted. We both smiled, shook hands, and moved on.

Chapter Ten
Look for Patterns

After lunch is a difficult time for Kiha. She struggles to settle down and often gets everyone riled up with her. I recommend putting her on noise patrol. Her job is to quiet everyone down after lunch. I once did this with a student. The first day on the job, he stood in the middle of my room and shouted, "Yo! Shut the f*ck up!" to the entire class.

Mortified, I pulled him aside and said, "Good job, good job, good job. Tomorrow, do the same thing, but this time, leave the F-bomb out."

The next day, he yelled, "Yo. Shut up!" Then it became, "Yo. Please shut up." Then, "Yo. Please shut up. Thank you." It took me over a month to teach him how to tell everyone to "shut the F up" appropriately. You tell me this should work because Kiha is a leader, though often in a negative way. The goal is for her to work *for* instead of *against* you. She influences everyone else. You need her more than she needs you is the mindset.

Look for patterns with kids. Is it the same time or scenario every day? I remember feeling so much anxiety as a kid when we did round robin reading. One person reads. The next person picks up where the first left off, and so on. As a struggling reader, I hated this activity because I never knew which passage was mine. It felt like a tidal wave coming around the room at me. Sometimes I would just knock everything off the desk just to distract my teacher. In my mind, everyone was going to laugh at me one way or another. I saw bad and stupid as the only two options. *If I can't read, well, they'll laugh at me for being dumb. Let me knock everything off the desk instead.*

A good rule to remember is kids who struggle or take longer to complete tasks don't usually like surprises. We don't like pop quizzes or tests. We don't like games where one person answers a question and randomly throws a ball to another person to answer the next question. If you are going to do activities like this, the struggling reader goes first. Give the exact passage they will read to them the day before so they can practice.

I'm asked what to do when a student disrupts during class. I tell the story of Jessup, one of my former students. In the middle of a lesson (that was not going well) he yelled, "Mr. Mendler, you have no idea what you're doing right now, do you?"

This, by the way, was the most on-task thing he said all year. I replied, "Actually no. Can you teach it better?"

He said, "I certainly couldn't teach it worse."

I threw him the whiteboard marker and he started teaching. He was good, so I sat in his seat and started disrupting class like he normally did. I drummed on the desk and rolled my eyes. He ignored and kept teaching. In fact, at one point, he walked over, got right in my ear and said, "Knock it off, Mr. Mendler," and walked away. He's not supposed to know how to do that.

After about five minutes, I stopped trying to disrupt

the class because I wasn't getting to him. Jessup taught for forty-three straight minutes. After class, I pulled him aside privately and said, "Yelling from across the room that I don't know what I'm doing is frustrating and I don't appreciate it. In the future, please do not embarrass me and I'll do the same. That said, you do have a career ahead of you in education if you choose." He said, "I know," and walked out. Teaching ability, yes. Social skills, not so much.

If there is a known catalyst making a student worse, be very careful doing that thing. Success must happen first. Focus on what I call the success cycle. Think of a clock without numbers. Where the 12 would normally be is the word success. Where the 3 would normally be is the word confidence. Where the 9 would normally be is the word competence. Think of a ball that spins between these three words, because in life, these words breed each other. Success breeds confidence. The more confident I am, the more competent I become, making me more successful. Many kids have never tasted any of the three. Sometimes we need to shove them into the cycle.

For example, tell the whole, "The homework tonight is numbers one to eleven odd. I will see all of them tomorrow. Have a great night."

Then pull Nicco aside and talk to him one-on-one. "Except for you. Tonight, please do number three only. When finished, check your answer against mine, making sure it is correct. Show up a few minutes early so I can check it over. Then you'll do it on the board in front of everyone."

The next day, he does it correctly in front of everyone. Walking back to his seat, subconsciously he starts thinking, *maybe math isn't so bad. Maybe I don't hate Mr. Mendler so much.*

The next night, I assign two through twelve even for the class. "Except for you, Nicco. Tonight, what do you think about doing numbers four and six? Check number four against mine to make sure it's correct. Try number six on your own. Good news is, it's exactly the same steps as number four. If you can do number four, you can definitely do number six." Success. Confidence. Competence.

Chapter Eleven

Helping Kids and Teachers Helping Each Other

This meeting is with social workers and counselors. They ask what to do when a student complains to them about other teachers. They ask how to change the teacher. I prefer changing kids instead of adults.

A student might tell me, "We hate that lady, Mr. Mendler. Admit it, you don't even like her either."

I reply, "What I think of her is irrelevant. I already passed math. That lady has something you need. It is called a grade. She holds it. Your job is to get it from her. I'm pretty sure the best way to get something you need from someone isn't by calling them names and saying how much you hate them. Do you want to have her again next year? That lady has failed dozens of kids before you and she will fail dozens after, but if you want to survive in her class, I will teach you how."

If the student says they don't care, I wish them luck and move on. I'm willing to give one hundred percent of my effort, but they have to meet me halfway.

Most are interested in learning what to do. When I taught high school, I hosted a "survival skills" class after school for kids who hated certain teachers but needed to survive in their classes.

During the March Madness basketball tournament, there is a phrase called "survive and advance." The goal is to win and move on. Whether it's by one point or twenty, it doesn't matter as long as you survive that game and advance to the next one. The same mentality applies here. My goal isn't to make them the best student in that class. It's for them to survive and move on to the next. We met every Wednesday after school. The class had one prerequisite to attend; you had to want to make a lot of money in your life. This was never a problem.

I started by asking kids to write or say out loud a list of all the professions a person can get rich doing. Of course, they said YouTubers, gamers, doctors, lawyers, athletes, and performers. This is actually a trick question, as the answer is any profession if you are the best at it. My good friend is a pilot. He flies a private plane for the CEO of a major company and is paid $500 thousand per year. The best plumber, the best electrician, and the best carpenter all make a lot of money. Just be great at whatever you do.

I wait for someone to say actor or actress. Next, they have to say or write down who their favorite is. Then I pick one. "Let's use Denzel Washington, Remember the Titans. Denzel was so good in that movie, he convinced you he was a football coach. To be clear, he never coached a down of football in his life before that movie. They don't pay people $25 million per movie unless you're really good at pretending to be something you're not. Your first role is pretending to like the teacher you hate."

The student will usually reiterate how much they hate that teacher again. My response is, "Right, and Sylvester Stallone isn't really Rocky or Rambo. He's Sylvester. Remember, we are pretending." At this point, a student will usually ask what exactly this means and how to do it. Then I explain the process.

"Step one is to say good morning to the teacher every day as soon as you walk in. Make eye contact and smile while saying it. Then sit down, and remember that you are not allowed to talk," I explain.

A student asks, "But what if she calls on me?"

I say, "She won't."

"But what if she does?" the kid insists.

"She won't," I repeat.

"But if she does?" the kid asks, yet again.

I say, "If she does, you can talk, but only if she calls on you. When she is teaching, she will make eye contact with you once in a while. When she does, step two is to smile and nod up and down. You don't need to know what she's talking about. Just pretend you do. Us teachers love kids who smile and nod when we teach. It makes us feel good about ourselves. Step three you're only going to do once a week. Every Thursday when class ends, walk up to her and say, 'I learned something today, thanks.' Then get out of there as fast as you can because if you stick around, she might ask what you learned."

Student says good morning and stops talking in class. Teacher becomes happy. Student smiles and nods, pretending he is interested. Teacher becomes happier. When I'm not sure how a seminar is going, I always look at the audience members who smile and nod. It gives me confidence. I know who they are, and I remember them later. They would always get the benefit of the doubt if I was scoring or grading them. Think about the last time a student stopped to say they learned something and thanked you for it. Every step of this process requires no extra school work from the student and is something they can always control. Really what I am doing is, with my invisible remote control over here, I am building a relationship between the student and teacher over there. It's a powerful process.

This backfired one time. My student Mike did this with a teacher and he came back to my room dejected. He said, "I did exactly what you said, and she yelled, 'stop being sarcastic' at me. As though there was nothing I could've learned in her class." That was the only time I went to a colleague and asked her to please play the game with him. Turn your focus to changing the kid instead of the other teachers.

Let students blow off steam in the counseling office. All of us need a safe place where we will not be judged. Explain how getting frustrated and angry actually gives the teacher what she wants. "Every time you lose control, the teacher wins. If you hold your temper, you are in control and you win." I like to use the words win, lose, control, and power. "Do you want to win in her room? Every time you call her a name, you lose control of yourself. She wins and you lose. Don't let her beat you. Stay in possession of your power at all times. When you get mad, she takes your power from you." Same mindset when a student is dealing with another student. At a staff meeting, counselors, psychologists, social workers, and support staff should explain the students' strengths to teachers. Many of us don't know how to best utilize them. Give occasional updates about kids. I realize you can't always be specific, but for example, you can say, "Hey everyone, Bobby is going through some really tough things at home. Please be extra compassionate this week. If you work with him directly, please come see me so I can fill you in a bit more. "

Communicate often and clearly with teachers, kids, and parents. One of the best things I ever did was have my counselor teach a lesson every Friday afternoon on a social issue kids were dealing with. At the time, I was sending kids to her instead of the office (the goal for them to return to class) for misbehavior. About two weeks in, she explained some were getting in trouble on purpose so they could see her. She suggested flipping it on them, bringing her to me. The kids loved it.

We discussed my thoughts on elementary kids switching classes. I am a fan. My fourth grader has two core teachers for two and a half hours every day. He loves it because he gets to meet more kids and learn from different people. They'll have bosses in life they don't like. Different personalities, styles, and rules are good. Switching also helps develop organizational skills. My daughter is in second grade, and she has one core teacher all day. She's also had a great year. Luckily, she loves her teacher and has a super strong bond with her. I still think it would have been good for her to switch. Focus on attitude and effort. Outcomes in life take care of themselves. But attitude and effort can always be controlled in every situation.

I also make clear that it's okay for kids to fail sometimes. Failure is a part of life. Failing because a student gives zero effort is different from failing because the work is too hard. Another counselor talks about a school sponsored trip taking kids to a professional hockey game and how it is viewed by some teachers as a reward for bad behavior. There are always two ways to look at things. Acknowledge their point because it does make sense to an extent. I don't agree with it, but I understand it. Then argue yours.

I think going to the game with kids and spending quality time connecting will directly transfer into better behavior and improved motivation in the classroom and school. At the end of the day, that's all I'm looking for. Plus, I can use the experience at the game to teach content. "Let's write a four-paragraph essay about our trip." Or, "If you have $25 to spend on food, and chicken tenders, fries, and a drink cost $12.50, how much do you have left?"

The good news is, my colleagues don't always have to agree with me. Teachers report to administrators, not other teachers. Everything does not always need to be explained or justified to everyone.

Chapter Twelve
Kids Who Leave Class and Have Trouble Connecting

Michael is their most difficult student. He was not there for most of class because he went to the bathroom. He was gone for fifteen minutes. He was supposed to be gone for two. This is often a problem. The aide was at lunch, so there was nobody to look for him. At the beginning of the year, he was gone three times a day for twenty to thirty minutes, so this is actually an improvement. This behavior is not just here, but happens in other classes as well.

He has a sheet or chart to keep track of goals set by counselors. He had some input creating the chart. This is good, as I believe kids should be part of creating and updating their behavior plan or IEP. Michael is given the sheet at the beginning of every day, and at the end of each class, the teacher gives comments and points based on how well he did. If he does not present the sheet, then there are no comments or points given. I recommend letting him rate and grade his own behavior (power and control). Then he compares his grade and rating to the teacher grade for him. They mutually agree on what he deserves.

Focus on teaching responsibility, which is only done by allowing kids to make decisions and live with the outcomes of the decisions they make. Remind him when he leaves class to keep track of his points. Have him say how long he will be out when leaving for the bathroom. You can even ask him what should happen if he's not back on time. Say, "I know this won't happen because you can be trusted, but if you are not back in five minutes, what should I do? If you were me, what would you do?"

Again, the goal is for him to take responsibility. Now instead of being annoyed that he took too long, I'm upset that he didn't keep his word on the amount of time he said he'd be gone. "Michael, I am really upset because I thought you were able to make decisions for yourself. Is this not true? You said five minutes and it became fifteen. Can I not trust you anymore? I'm annoyed that at the age of twelve," (or whatever the student's age is), "you don't stick to what you say. That bothers me way more than you not coming back on time."

Notice I'm not emphasizing him being gone for too long. My issue is him not being able to make decisions and keep his word.

There are close to fifty items on Michael's behavior sheet for him to improve. *Stay in your seat, bring a pen, do not disturb others,* and *raise your hand* are just a few. Many items are well written, but many others are broad, subjective, and leave room for argument. Remember, respect means different things to different people, making it a value. Values answer why expectations are put in place. Value equals respect. Based on that, valuing the rule and expectation equals hands and feet to yourself. Notice the expectation is specific, measurable, and tells what to do.

This is evident in our society. The expectation when driving is specific; driving 65 miles per hour is the limit while driving 66 miles per hour is speeding. You don't have to like or agree with it, but it can't be argued. Pick one thing at a time to work on. When he masters that, move to the next. He gets a say in deciding which one to work on first. With Michael, try to predict and preempt by using questions instead of statements.

"I'm thinking about checking the camera, what do you think I'll see? If you did hit another student, what should be done? Should there be a consequence?" Pick a day, and from the minute you wake up in the morning until the minute you go to bed at night, no matter what anyone does, no matter what anyone says, only use questions.

"What's the homework gonna be?" a student asks.

"Great question," I reply. "What do you think it should be? You think ten problems? Fifteen? How about I give you twenty and you pick whatever five you want?"

A kid asks, "How much longer do we have to do this?"

I reply with, "How much longer can you focus? How about eight on-task minutes, then eight head-down minutes? Thoughts? Can you keep track of how many minutes or should I? I'm sure this won't happen, but if you choose not to pick your head up after eight minutes, what should I do?" Questions force students to look internally and often get them to make the same decisions we would make for them anyway. Also, ask your student if there is something you can work on as well to be a better teacher for them. Hold each other accountable.

We discuss the difference between success in school and success in life. I believe they are totally different. Success in school means being really good at many different things: math, science, ELA, foreign language, physical education, music, art, etc. To be successful in real life, that same person has to be great at one thing. I've never gone to the dentist and asked the hygienist to tell me the causes of World War II before my cleaning. Just clean my teeth and do it right. I don't care what else you know how to do. If you fly the plane I am on, get me up and get me down and do it in the right place. Again, I don't care what else you're good at. Ask students to think about what their one thing in life will be. Don't be afraid to praise Michael just for showing up. For some students, life is easier when distant and guarded. They are afraid to get close to adults because of a deep fear of being hurt. This is often the root of the problem. Tell him what the problem is and that you understand it probably better than he does.

For example: "You have moved five times and been in three different schools. You're not interested in connecting with adults because you don't trust us. I'd be exactly the same way if I were you. I think it's incredible that you come to school every day. It isn't right that you've moved so much. But just so you know, I'm not going anywhere. Even if you move again I will check on you. I will follow up. I will be here. Once a person comes into my life, it's really hard for them to get out. So get used to me."

Michael might tell you this is not true. Just say, "Okay. But if you ever do want to talk about it, I'm here." Then move on. As always, this is done as privately as possible.

Another suggestion is for Michael to keep a personal mini notebook. At the end of each day or class, (or even hour or fifteen minutes), he writes one positive statement about himself. The teacher can add to this if he or she wants. We conclude by remembering behaviors are never the problem. They are always solutions kids pick to their problems of attention, power, control, competence, and belonging. For Michael, it's abandonment and a combination of the above five. Focus on the foundation of the problem (cause) rather than the symptom (effect), and usually you will see change.

They ask what to do when students complain about their grade. I teach them a strategy called "take a shot," perfect for my future lawyers and sales reps. Students get two minutes or less to convince me I'm wrong about something. Don't like a grade? Convince me it should be different. Mad about a consequence? Cool, change my mind. If they're uncomfortable speaking, they can write their shot.

When I taught fourth grade, I watched a girl kick a boy right in front of me. I decided she was not allowed to go on the field trip. Her shot went like this: "Okay, Mr. Mendler. I admit I kicked him. I did it and I shouldn't have. That's what you call taking responsibility, right? But here's the thing. I was gonna kick him like five other times and I didn't. Isn't that what you call self-control? You love baseball, Mr. Mendler. In baseball, if I was up ten times and got nine hits, would it be a good game or bad? I feel like I was nine for ten, so I should be allowed to go." Then she turned and walked away. I have to admit, it was an excellent shot. Whether I let her go is not the point. The point is, sometimes we see the same thing very differently than they do. In my mind, she kicked someone. In her mind, she used self-control. It's always interesting to see each situation through student eyes.

Chapter Thirteen
Praise with Passion

We start by talking about how hard it is when students like Cheyenne don't take medication. Often near the end of the month, her mom sells it for drug money. Talk to her about how it feels not to have her medicine. Does she feel different? Did she talk to you about her parents selling it? How does this make her feel? Talk about yourself to her. Relationships mean I learn about my students, and they learn about me. Focus on attitude and effort. Her mom reads at a fourth grade level and is not interested in Cheyenne becoming successful. Cheyenne is not afraid of anyone or anything. Homework is generally a problem because her parents can't do it, so it rarely gets done. Stop giving it. Instead, just get as much as you can from her in class. Once in a while, give homework to the few who might do it. Homework is nothing more than a vehicle to a destination. Focus on the destination (what the student is supposed to learn from the homework). Deliver the content to her world. If Cheyenne had one hour after school to do whatever she pleased, what would she pick? Go to her island. Bring some content over instead of forcing her to yours. Focus on what she needs to learn more than what you are supposed to teach. Stay focused on what you can control. You don't control if she is disrespectful to you. You do control how you respond. It's easy to be respectful to respectful people. Anyone can do that. The question is, am I able to be respectful when someone disrespects me? Focus on building relationships, getting to know her, and teaching social skills. Teach "please" and "thank you" and how to say, "good morning." Focus on how to shake a hand and job interviewing skills. Teach kids how to act interested when bored. Remember to have fun. When feeling burnout, think about what got you into this profession. Go back to that and make it your focal point.

The teacher is excited to tell me about growth made with another student. She was struggling to connect but found out he enjoys acting and drama. He loves getting in front of the class to do math, but hates doing it on paper. He's a good actor and is funny, so this makes sense. Work at feeding him a healthy dose of attention every day as often as possible. Get in his ear and let him know what an amazing job he does on basic things. "I love how you walked in this classroom today. Great job walking in. You walk in on time every day in all classes and good things will happen for you." Praise with as much passion and energy as you correct. Some kids learn the only way to get noticed is to be inappropriate.

Focus on attention. Be relentless with this. When he's inappropriate, do your best to ignore the behavior, then privately praise him as soon as it stops. "Great job stopping. I'm proud of you. Yesterday you were inappropriate for twelve straight minutes, but today it was only seven. Awesome job."

Anxiety usually has a negative effect on performance. There are exceptions, but for the most part, anxiety makes us worse at whatever we do. I can usually hit a golf ball relatively straight, but line up a bunch of spectators like they do at the Masters, and someone will probably get killed. Grip gets tighter. Hands start to sweat. Performance is affected. This is why it makes no sense to add a giant dose of anxiety before kids do something important.

The teacher asks what to do with struggling readers. First, take the pressure off. I remember a high school teacher once telling me reading was overrated. He said, "You have to know how to do it, but you don't have to be great at it. You have to read the board in an airport or signs on the highway, but don't worry if you struggle with certain words." This was the opposite message I was used to hearing. With the explosion of podcasts, audio books, and satellite radio, this holds truer today.

I often misbehaved before having to do something that was uncomfortable or difficult. Address discomfort with the student. Let them know that when they feel it, it's okay, and you will be right beside them to help push them through it. Remind them that discomfort equals growth in the world. Share a personal story of when you pushed through something hard. Always try to relate. Get creative. Many teachers ask kids to read the book first, and if time warrants, watch the movie. This is great for the majority of kids. For the struggling reader, I prefer the opposite. Watch the video or movie first. When finished, read the book. We discuss the difference between movies (have a time limit) and books (no time limit). When reading something that is not in the movie, stop and discuss. Ask questions like, "Should this be in the movie, and if so, what do you take out?"

In general, strugglers do not like academic surprises. "I am randomly calling on someone" should not be random. Be careful creating an environment where certain students can look bad in front of the class, with things like pop quizzes, tests, or games. Again, I'm not saying not to do these things. I'm saying for certain kids, be sure to rig their experience so they don't look bad in front of others. Try hard to stay mentally strong. Don't let pressures from what you are supposed to teach (from administration and the state) get in the way of what kids actually need to learn. Always go with need over supposed to when feeling the tear.

Use the two-question teacher evaluation:
1. What are two things you really like about me as a teacher?
2. What are two things you do not like about me as a teacher?

I assure them they cannot get in trouble nor will I get mad or defensive, no matter what they answer.

"Mr. Mendler, we love you, there is nothing we would change," one student says.

"Great. I guess you will get fifty percent on the quiz," I say.

"Mr. Mendler, we hate you!" another student says.

"Great. I guess you'll get fifty percent on the quiz. No matter how much you love someone in this world, there are always two things they can improve. Vice versa is also true. No matter how much you hate someone, there are always two things you can find that they do well."

Chapter Fourteen
But First, Success

Alex Snyder is quiet for the most part. Not defiant, not disruptive, and not rude. He just flies under the radar. The special education teacher in this inclusion class, Jennifer, can't get the time of day from him. My guess is it's a special education issue. He probably wants no part of anyone thinking he is a special ed kid. The more Jennifer tries, the more Alex pushes away. If she checks on what he's doing, Alex shuts down. For now, Jennifer leaves him alone and Alex gets work done. Good move. Leave him alone in class. Let him do his work.

Outside of class is different. Practice the two by ten technique; two uninterrupted moments for ten consecutive days. The only goal is connection. Catch him in the hall where there's no stigma. Jennifer has tried, but Alex acts the same. When pressed, she admits she hasn't actually timed how long she's talked to him and has not done ten consecutive days. That said, if Alex is not bothering others and gets work done, I'm not sure what the big deal is.

Jennifer asks if Alex is disrespectful by ignoring her. Nothing is disrespectful unless we decide it is. If you decide it isn't, then it isn't. If kids are learning, nothing else matters. Everything else is secondary. A huge benefit of inclusion is multiple teachers. If a student doesn't click with one, there's another. If Alex stops working or becomes defiant, you can adjust.

Remember the success cycle from earlier? Success breeds confidence, which breeds competence, which makes me more successful. Sometimes we have to shove a student in by feeding something that guarantees success. There's a reason little kids start by playing T-ball. We put the ball on a tee. That's not baseball. In fact, it's not even close, but we all agree to do it because we understand success has to come first. Then there's graduation from T-ball to underhand coach pitch. Have you ever been the coach or parent pitching? You're not actually trying to throw a strike. You're literally trying to hit the bat. Why? Because success has to come first. More success equals more confidence, making a person better (more competent) at whatever they do. Then it's an overhand pitch, thrown like a dart again, with the goal to hit the bat. Eventually, if you've done it correctly, the day comes where you go out back and plan to do it the same way. Except, all of a sudden, your kid says, "No Mom, no Dad, no Coach. Back up and throw it harder. You aren't throwing it hard enough. I know I can hit it," but not if we never put the ball on a tee. Some kids are trying to hit 90-mile an hour fastballs, but they've never played tee ball.

They ask my opinion of kids who do nothing. I say let them as long as they are not disturbing others. Call me cocky or arrogant, but I believe a student doing nothing in my room is better than nothing somewhere else in my building, if I see those as the only two options. I believe

I'm good enough that, at some point, I'll say or do something that will get him to look up. If he's not here, I don't even get that chance. Eventually, they will hopefully pay attention to something that interests them.

I'm not saying I want a student to do nothing. But sometimes there's no other option. Focus on attitude and effort and connecting your content to their interests. What do they like? Go to their island and then glance back at yours to see what you can bring over. Every time a student responds with "I don't know," my response is, "Pretend you knew. If you did, what would you say then?"

"But I said I don't know," they reply.

"Right, we got that, and there are tons of things in the world I don't know either. But let's have some fun and pretend. If you did know, what would you say?"

The same thing applies when a kid says, "I don't care." I say, "Pretend you cared. If you did, what would you say then?"

"But I said I don't care," they reply.

"I know, and there are lots of things I don't care about either. There are also lots of things I do care about. For this one, pretend you cared. What would you say then?"

This works for spouses as well. "Honey, where would you like to go for dinner tonight?"

My wife might say, "I don't care."

I respond with, "Pretend you cared. If you did, what would you say?"

"Cheesecake Factory," she replies.

"Perfect. Let's go."

I remind teachers to be careful turning their backs on kids. Try hard to position yourself at a point in the room where you can see everyone at all times. If this isn't possible, get some small (preferably unbreakable) mirrors and strategically place them around the room. Some kids here need to work on manners.

"Yo, let me get a pencil" is not the proper way to ask for something. Ask him to ask again. This time, it's, "May I please borrow a pencil?" After giving it to him, make sure he says thank you. If he doesn't, take the pencil back until he does. This works both ways. Be sure you always use manners when asking them to do something. It's not okay for me to say, "Okay, everyone, take out your books" or "I need you all to sit down." If I expect manners and appropriateness from them, they can expect the same from me.

Chapter Fifteen
Changing Behaviors Is Hard

The teacher tells me about a second period student that says "your mama" all the time, swears at kids, and writes on other people's papers. She's like this in other classes and doesn't have any friends because of it. Sometimes she gives attitude to the teacher. Some days are great, and others she won't try. Basically, her day is a roller coaster ride. This is normal for kids and adults. If you see this pattern, you're on the right track. Don't get off. We talked about it earlier; this is the natural progression for change. Have you ever tried changing something about yourself? Were you totally successful the first time you tried? Probably not. Usually it takes time to change, and this is when we are adults and already motivated.

Frequently, we have good days, bad days, or good hours and bad hours. Sometimes it's a good ten minutes, sometimes it's a bad ten minutes. During the down cycle of my roller coaster ride in my life, from the people closest to me, I need support, love, understanding, commitment, dedication, and honesty. It never benefits me during my down cycle for the people closest to me to punish. In life, when things go bad, most people scatter.

Two hundred and fifty people show up for the wedding. How many of those same people came for the divorce?

Things go wrong in life and it's hard to find anyone. They fly in from all over the world for the open bar, don't they? Good news for me is I never liked going with traffic anyway. In fact, I hate traffic. Normally in life, if you see everyone going one way, I'm going the other.

Now that we know this and are aware of it, we see the kid differently. He has a good Monday and a good Tuesday. I expect a bad Wednesday. Hopefully I'm wrong, but I brace because Monday and Tuesday were so good. Day three of going to the gym is often harder than day one. Day five of a diet is harder than day three. Nobody likes a storm, but we like it much better when we see it coming from miles away and are prepared for it. Now all heck breaks loose Wednesday. While everyone else scatters, I sneak in.

I tell the student, "I'm not happy with your behavior. It's not okay to hit. It's not okay to kick. It's not okay to spit. It's not okay to bite, and it's unacceptable to call people names. I'm very unhappy that you did those things. I also want to tell you how incredible Monday and Tuesday were. Both were fantastic days, and right now you and I are going to sit in this spot and not move until we figure out how tomorrow will be more like yesterday than it was like today. What happened yesterday that didn't happen today? What happened today that didn't happen yesterday?"

"Well, for one thing, yesterday my mom was home and today she wasn't," the kid says.

"What do you mean your mom wasn't home?" I ask.

"How many meanings does that have, sir? She

wasn't home," the student replies.

"Got it. What happens when she isn't home?"

"My older brother has to get me and my little sister ready for school. He has to pack our lunches and make sure we have all our stuff. Also, on these days, my brother automatically misses school or is late," the student explains.

"Why is that?"

"Because in almost every school, including ours, the high school starts way earlier than the elementary school. So if he stays home to help us, he misses his bus. Everyone at the high school thinks he's a bad kid but he's not a bad kid. He's a good kid. Also, the whole time we are worried about my mom. One other thing is, you know the lady that stands out front every morning with the walkie talkie? She always says hi to everyone. Yesterday she was out there and today she wasn't."

"Why does that matter so much?" I inquire.

"Because she notices stuff."

"What do you mean she notices stuff?"

"Like when your shoe can be untied. Some teachers will yell from across the whole bus loop, 'Hey! Your shoe's untied!' That's not what she does," the kid explains.

"Really? What does she do?" I ask.

"She comes over to you all private and gets down on your level. Then with a huge smile she quietly says, 'Good morning. It's so good to see you. I know we are both going to have great days. I was going to tell you that your shoe is untied but before I do (and you don't even have to answer this), it looks like you haven't eaten this morning. If so, go to my room. Second drawer on the left, I have granola bars, apples, and bananas. Take what

you want. By the way, give me that shoe real quick.'
And, Mr. Mendler, man, she ties one of them crazy knots.
Not one of the ones that comes undone but one of the
ones that cuts off the circulation in your foot. Well,
yesterday she was out there and today she wasn't."

"I heard everything you just said, and I feel awful
that your mom didn't come home, and I don't think it's
right," I say.

"Are you saying you don't like my mom?"

"Not at all. I like your mom very much. I also
disagree with some choices she makes, but I think if she
knew every choice I made, she wouldn't agree with all of
them either. She just doesn't know every choice I make.
As for the lady who stands out front; I know exactly who
you're talking about. She's great and we need to do a
better job of making sure someone's out there if she can't
be. I think sometimes we do a bad job paying attention
to what matters most to you, and we have to be better.
That said, I have to push back a little because everything
you just said fundamentally breaks the number one rule
that we have in this classroom. 'Every time in my life I
have a problem with someone or something, I am at least
part of the cause of that problem.' You just said you
haven't seen your mom in twenty-four hours, correct?
But it's her fault that you're biting, kicking, punching,
spitting, and hitting? Please explain how it's her fault."

"Well, it's not," the student admits.

"Right. Whose fault is it?"

"Mine."

"Correct," I confirm. "Because the truth is,
whether or not your mother ever comes home again or
that lady is ever outside again, you never have the right to
bite, kick, punch, spit, and hit. Those things are not okay.

The good news for you is that biting, kicking, punching, spitting, and hitting aren't your problems. They're solutions you've chosen to your problems. Your real problems are anger, annoyance, aggravation, and frustration, and the crazy thing is, those things will be with you for the rest of your life. They'll never go away. Remember the rule I wrote about earlier? 'If it feels amazing in the short term, it's usually really bad for me in the long term and vice versa. If it hurts a lot short term, it's usually really good for me long term.' Biting, kicking, punching, spitting, and hitting all feel good in the short term, no doubt. I take boxing lessons myself because it feels good to hit something sometimes. But when you hit another person in school, think about what happens. You get in trouble, your parents get called, you get suspended, you miss more school, and you get farther behind. The only person you hurt is yourself."

This conversation takes time and work. I have to go out of my way to have it. There are usually other things I could be doing. Invest the time, anyway. Always try to figure out which need (attention, power, control, competence, or belonging) is most lacking. Name calling, cussing, and disrupting others are all symptoms of a kid screaming for attention. Yank the behavior out at the root. Remember to control attitude and effort at all times. Keep trying to connect, as it is never okay to quit on a student. I ask how much time she spends outside of class building relationships with kids from this class. None. Go out and find them even when they are not required to be with you. This can be done at lunch, during free periods, before school, in hallways, and after school. See it as an investment. I promise it will be worth it.

Chapter Sixteen
Behavior Charts

I notice a behavior chart on the wall. Each student's name is across the top of the chart on a cut-out airplane. Across the bottom are three categories for behavior: smooth ride, turbulence, and crash. Out of thirty-one students on the wall, twenty-seven are smooth, three turbulent, and one crashed. The teacher tells me, "Yeah twenty-seven of them are good all the time. They're never the problem."

My answer is, "Why do you have a chart for them? You just told me they're always good. That's like giving twenty-seven people wheelchairs when they walk perfectly fine."

He asks, "Okay, well then what do I do?"

"First, please get the chart off the wall. Student behavior is not a decoration for a classroom. On one hand, we tell kids non-stop all day to mind their own business. Then we put a behavior chart on the wall for all to see. We don't get it both ways. Either we want them to mind their own business, or we don't. Now that it's off the wall, for twenty-seven of them, we do nothing. Because they walk perfectly fine. You said it yourself. They're always smooth. Let's look at the remaining four.

Three turbulent and one crashed," I say.

I then ask him to tell me about each of the four. The first struggles sitting still. Up, down, up, down, in and out of his seat all day. He gets a chart between him, his parents, and the teacher, and nobody else will focus on whether or not he's sitting still in his seat. If he's up fifteen times a day, the goal is ten. At the end of every hour (or class period) he tells the teacher how he did instead of the teacher telling him. The goal is for him to take responsibility for his own behavior. Do the same with each student that's turbulent or crashes.

Focus on one behavior at a time. Now instead of a generic chart on the wall for everyone that's public, embarrassing, and fixes no one, we have individual charts for individual kids based on individual things they struggle with.

A girl volunteers an answer and it's incorrect. You say, "Nope. Anyone else want to try?" I'm not sure you notice the look on her face. Her eyes shoot down and her smile turns to a frown. Instead, try saying, "Great guess, and I totally see your thoughts. In fact, I think a lot of people here probably thought the same thing. Thanks for taking a chance. Does anyone have a different guess?"

It takes skill to tell a kid they're wrong and have them feel good about themselves at the same time. Making someone feel good while failing or struggling can have a huge impact on classroom management and culture. It's easy to forget to praise kids for doing what they're supposed to do. The more we praise, the more we can criticize. One doesn't work without the other. If I'm always criticizing, I become predictable.

"Here comes Mr. Mendler again, always telling me what I did wrong." Their guard is immediately up. I deliver my message and it bounces off. I often hear teachers say, "I don't get what the problem is. I've told him the same thing like twenty times this year. When will he learn?"

Telling him the same thing twenty times is the problem. Every once in a while, mix in a curveball because your fastball is getting rocked. When the student anticipates criticism, walk over and deliver a big fat compliment instead to catch him off guard. Now I can criticize again the next day because his guard is down. Remember, the second to last word is best.

Let's discuss Kayden. He seems desperate for attention as well, but also craves power and control. This often comes from a home life of feeling like he's in complete control and in charge. He stays up until all hours, no screen-time limits, eats on the floor while watching TV (and it magically gets cleaned up). This student comes to school holding on tight to the little bit of power and control he feels. Then the teacher tries taking it from him by constantly telling him what to do. The goal is to get him on your side.

I'm the head coach of this classroom (my name is on the door, remember?) and he's my first assistant. Frequently check in with him. Ask for his opinion. "How many questions should be on the test? I was thinking twenty. What do you think? Want to help me decide which review game to play? What do you think about this seating arrangement I planned?"

During these interactions, continue to build a relationship with him. Connect by being vulnerable. Share your story (especially the parts that might be similar to his). Figure out ways for him to take care of you. I often joke with people that the best way to lose weight is to put a scale in the classroom. Every day the class gets to weigh you and write the number under "do not erase" on the board. No better way to accomplish something than to hold ourselves accountable to students.

When we view the behavior as just a symptom, it allows the teacher to stay calm and focused in the moment. If you're really at your wits' end with him, utilize other adults. My school psychologist friend, Mr. Kilgore, and I had a secret system. If a student entered his office from my room holding the book *A Lesson Before Dying*, it meant I needed a fifteen-minute break. I wasn't mad. I didn't want him written up or in trouble. I just needed a break. I also had a bright orange pass in my room that meant strangulation thoughts were entering my mind (kidding, mostly). This pass meant he needed to hold the student longer.

Chapter Seventeen
Winning Over Your #1 Trouble Maker

Christina begins by telling me her entire class is out of control. She's frazzled and flustered, having just come from her most difficult class. Most upsetting to me is that she allowed students to get her this upset. Think about mental toughness. The only reason you are so annoyed is because you are trying to teach something, and the students are in the way. Remember earlier when we discussed the delivery world? We need to leave our island and go to theirs. What are they interested in? What do they like? In their spare time, what do they choose to do?

After helping Christina see that the first person she must work on is herself, we discuss the kids. I never believe an entire class is out of control. Sometimes it looks that way, but all groups have leaders. We need to figure out who they are and how to get them on our side. Leaders are usually able to influence others. Think about, "When X is absent I can get everyone else to behave. Okay, fine, X and Y."

Christina says, "No, it is X, Y, and Z. Actually, when X and Y are gone, Z isn't bad. I think X is really the one." In the span of a few minutes, we went from "an entire class that is completely out of control" to just one or two kids. Mentally, it's much easier to change one or two than to change twenty-two. If I get those two on my side, they already control everyone else. Give them as many opportunities to be in charge. Find ways for them to feel power and control. Is there someone or somewhere else in the school for them to help? Ask their opinion before doing an activity. "Should we read this book or that book? When finished, should I ask these questions or those questions? Would you like to help me write some questions?"

The teacher says she does this, but some kids complain that it isn't fair if one student gets more jobs and tasks than others.

Teach them what it means to be fair. In my room, fair means every person gets what they need to be successful. I say to my students, "I promise to always do my best to be fair to each of you, which means I also promise not to always treat you all exactly the same way. So that I can be fair."

"What do you mean?" a student asks.

"Good question," I say. "You might get ten problems for homework and your best friend might only get two. I'm not saying that will happen, I'm just saying it might. If it does, neither of you will complain that I'm not being fair. You might complain I'm not treating you all exactly the same way, but I don't promise to treat you the same way. That way, I can be fair."

"I am still confused," the kid replies.

"Two of you might do the same inappropriate behavior. One might get one consequence and the other a totally different consequence, or no consequence at all. Again, I'm not saying that will happen, I'm just saying it might. If it does, please don't complain that I'm not being fair. You can complain I'm not treating you exactly the same way, but I'm not promising to treat you exactly the same way. That's what makes it fair."

Explain this to parents as well. "I will always do my best to be fair to each and every one of your children. However, I will not always treat them exactly the same way. One might get ten problems and another five. One might get one consequence, and another might get something different for the same exact behavior. Please don't complain that it's not fair."

It's so important to be upfront and honest about how things will work with kids and their parents. If applicable, share a relevant story. For example, I have a sister fourteen years younger than me. We often hung out on Friday nights and would order a large pizza with ten slices. Being fair means we both eat until we are full. If I eat five slices and she eats three, I don't rip her mouth open and say, "Lisa, you need to eat two more because I ate five and being fair means you need to eat five as well." This would be totally ridiculous. Fair means we both get what we need in that moment to be successful, or in this case, full.

The teacher agrees content-focused lessons should be put on hold once in a while to really work with kids' needs (supposed to vs. need). Talk to them about their lives. Tell them about yours. What things do you struggle with? How have you overcome them? Ask questions about family, friends, and relationships. Help guide them through problems at home with suggestions and advice. Be vulnerable. Tell them a struggle you have in your life and ask them to hold you accountable. We spend a lot of time helping kids, and rightfully so. But think about it in reverse. If I'm always on the receiving end of help, I become helpless. That's what helplessness is. When we flip this, and the kids always getting helped become the helpers, we often see a change in kids like no other. Remember why you went into this profession in the first place and draw back on that. Did you go in because you love grades and standards, or because you wanted to help kids? The ability to do it is still there every day. Make that your focus.

Chapter Eighteen
Teach Behaviors You Want to See

We discuss a wide range of topics, including behavior plans, rule enforcement, self-contained students switching classes, inclusion, and consistency. It's fine to have a behavior plan for individual kids if it is needed. I explain that, not only is it okay for teachers to have different rules and consequences, but it's actually beneficial. A couple years ago, I was working at Caesars Palace in Las Vegas. I went to eat at the sports bar the night before my workshop, and a man started smoking a cigarette three seats away from me. I asked the bartender if she was going to do anything about it.

She said to me, "Sir, what's your problem?"

I said, "My problem? That guy is smoking inside."

She said, "Yes. He is."

I didn't realize in Nevada you can smoke inside (apparently secondhand smoke is not an issue there). In New York, thirty years ago we figured out secondhand smoke can kill people. Thus, you cannot smoke at all indoors. Apparently Nevada hasn't figured this out yet. But Nevada didn't change their law because Brian was visiting. I had to adjust to them. I believe the best schools are run like the United States government was originally designed; individual classrooms and teachers being treated like states. For the most part, each creates its own rules, policies, and guidelines. The federal government (administration) creates policies and rules directly pertaining to safety. Other than that, individual teachers make decisions and policies as they see fit. Obviously the main office offers input and suggestions and keeps a close eye on "states" that struggle most.

The topic of headphones comes up, and across the board, teachers tell me they don't understand why kids are not allowed to wear them. I agree and explain many examples of students using headphones to learn. Since headphones do not usually pertain to safety, they should be an individual "state" issue. In a self-contained classroom, it's important teachers have every possible tool at their disposal. This does not mean they have to allow headphones. It just means individual teachers get to make the call depending on the circumstances in that room at that time.

We spend a good amount of time discussing teaching behaviors you want to see. A teacher says that students often come to her room when they are not technically in her class. She says she immediately sends them back. I agree to a point. However, it's important to teach that student *how* to behave in the class they are sent from. It's the student's job to adjust to the "state" they are in at that time. However, many need help doing so. See "survival skills" from earlier in the book.

The message should not just be, "You're not supposed to be in my room right now, so you have to leave." Once the appropriate behaviors have been taught and practiced, it's reasonable for teachers to enforce a student being where she's supposed to be at all times. Transitions are difficult for some kids because they're used to being in one room with one teacher all day.

I ask the staff to participate in an activity with me, and I invite you to do the same. Close your eyes and think about something specific you're really good at in your life. It can be anything, but it has to be specific. For example, you can't just say sports, or cooking, or art. You have to say golfing, or making lasagna, or painting portraits. Think about the first time you ever did this. Were you really good the first time? How about the second time? How did you get better? Getting good at anything starts with first becoming comfortable in that environment. Once you're comfortable, it takes the cycle of practice, patience, and guidance. In school we often do the opposite. We "contain" kids that are not good at walking in the hall. We say, "You don't know how to behave on the playground, so you'll be inside with me during recess." Or, "You continue to show you don't know how to behave appropriately on the bus, so you're not going on the field trip." The only place to improve at golf is on the golf course. The only place to improve at cooking is in the kitchen. The only place to improve at walking in the hallway is in the hallway. The only place to improve on the bus is on the bus. Try hard not to take away behaviors kids actually need most. Remember, predictability is so important. Of course transitions are going to be difficult at first. The more kids struggle, the more practice we need to do on the skill they struggle with.

Many complain about kids not getting to class on time. Use teasers to get them excited. What will they miss if they're late? Make the first five minutes of class so good they can't imagine not being there. Explain why being on time matters in life and begin the lesson immediately, even if all students are not present. I'm not sure why so many teachers wait for everyone to sit quietly and pay attention before beginning. These same people seem to always be waiting. Be in charge of your room. This means starting when it's time to start. This also means some might not be ready. They will catch up. Have a specific, detailed agenda on the board broken down by times. Don't worry about sticking to it all the time, but allow it to guide you. When class ends, give a quick explanation of where you plan to start the next day. Of course everything is subject to change depending on student issues and teachable seconds.

I say teachable seconds because there is really no such thing as a teachable moment. There are split-second decisions I have to make. I wish there were sixty full seconds to decide which direction to go. Like in football, the running back gets the handoff from the quarterback. The play was designed to go left. It went left in practice all week and worked. The coach wants it to go left. The running back takes a step left, and there are three defenders in the backfield. There aren't sixty seconds to decide if he should cut back and go the other way. There's no time to ask permission from the coach first. Players must have confidence to audible at the line of scrimmage. Teachers in school are the players. Administrators are coaches. I'm the one getting tackled if the play doesn't go right, which means I get to make the final call. We need to have the confidence from administrators that if we audible and throw a pick six, they'll still applaud us for being willing to do what we thought was best.

Correct and praise kids as often, privately, and intensely as possible. One of my favorite acronyms is called PEP. This stands for privacy, eye contact, and proximity. Privacy and proximity are the most important. Eye contact is good too, if possible, but don't force that on kids. Say what you need to say and move. "I love that shirt, it looks great on you, keep wearing that color." Or, "Knock it off, enough is enough, please stop!" Both done as quickly and privately as possible.

I recently taught this at a live seminar, and a lady in the back called out, "I don't move very well physically."

Before I could respond, a lady in front yelled, "Then move mentally."

The one in back yelled back, "How do you do that?"

The one in front said, "I don't know, go ask half the people that are married in this country. Don't tell me you can't be one place physically and another mentally. I've done it for twenty-three straight years."

I'd hate to be her husband.

On Fridays around noon, most of us start going to another place mentally. Same with Sunday nights. Mental toughness is the single most important component to being a great teacher, and I have a couple of favorite acronyms that help with this. One is HALTS, which stands for hungry, angry, lonely, tired, and scared. Anger is what we will see from the student. I can't fix another person's anger, but I can help with hunger, loneliness, tiredness, and fear, all of which usually cause anger. Another is HOPE, which stands for hearing other people's experiences, reminding me to really focus on listening to kids. ABT stands for always be teaching. NBP stands for never be punishing.

Chapter Nineteen
Rewards and Accepting Late Work

A teacher asks about incentives and rewards for good behavior and staying awake. I think individual rewards often cause aggravation and frustration. The same kids frequently win, and others are left out. I also think there's a big difference between a bribe and a reward. Bribes happen before a behavior, and rewards happen after. For example, if I say to my son Eli, "If you do a really good job at karate, I'll get you a donut after," I'm bribing him because the behavior (him doing a good job at karate) didn't happen yet. A reward would be if he already did a really good job, and because of it, I decided to give him a donut after without him knowing or asking.

To be clear, I'm not saying never to bribe. Bribing is better than chaos, so if you have chaos, then bribe. That said, it shouldn't be enough. Bribes will get you good behavior in the presence of authority, but that's not what I'm looking for. I'm not on the bus. I'm not on the playground. I'm not in the cafeteria. When I was a kid, before a sleepover my parents used to make it very clear: "You behave better at the neighbor's house than you do at ours."

Using rewards privately is best. Don't have an assembly or get on the loudspeaker. Just drop by a desk, table, or area and give them something extra when nobody is looking. I prefer rewarding everyone in honor of one. Pretend you're in first grade and I'm your teacher. I say to the class, "Hey, everyone, I'm so proud of Jennifer. Her behavior has been amazing this week. Because she's been so great, she gets two free homework passes."

Are you happy for her? Possibly. There's also a good chance you're annoyed and might say, "She behaves for one week and gets rewarded? I'm good all the time and the teacher doesn't notice me."

Or even worse, if you want to have students really annoyed at each other, you could say, "Jennifer has been amazing this week. She has worked really hard on her behavior. Because she has been so good, Jennifer gets to pick any two friends she wants for an extra fifteen minutes on the playground. Quickly, Jenny, pick two people."

Jenny picks two, and you aren't one of them. Later at lunch or on the bus, you might approach her and say, "But I thought I was your best friend. I picked you last week and you didn't even pick me this week? Whatever."

When I was a kid, it was, "I don't care anyway. I don't even like the playground and I really dislike the name Jenny." Why put her in this position if not necessary? The fix is simple. Instead of rewarding only Jenny, reward the entire class in honor of her.

"Because I'm so proud of Jenny, and she's behaved so well this week, each of you get an extra fifteen minutes on the playground in honor of her. Don't thank me because I had nothing to do with it. In fact, if it were up to me, there are a few of you that still would not be allowed to participate. But because of Jenny, everyone means everyone. Thank her, not me."

Then if you feel the need, when nobody is looking, you may privately hand Jenny something else. I don't think she needs it because everyone getting rewarded in her honor is enough. Don't make a big scene and don't have an assembly to announce it. Just quickly and privately give her something extra if need be. Also, try to reward kids with feelings instead of stuff. Make them feel hopeful. Make them feel excitement. Make them feel happiness. Stuff gets lost, stolen, and broken. Feelings last.

A teacher asks if she should accept late work. This reminds me of my first year teaching seventh grade inclusion ELA. I was the SPED teacher and Mr. Decamp was the Gen Ed teacher. In the middle of March, a boy named Devion said to me, "Mr. Mendler, here's my summer reading assignment." Please understand this paper was due the first week of September. He's handing it to me six months later. I smiled and said, "You're kidding right? You think you can just hand a paper in six months late? No chance. Out."

Devion groaned and began walking out. Mr. Decamp, from across the room, said, "Dev, hold on a second. Mr. Mendler here is in his first year. He obviously has never been taught how to take a late paper. Hand it to me so I can teach him."

I thought to myself, *Oh sh*t*. This man never missed a teachable second with kids or adults. I didn't like him at the time, but discomfort is the only way to grow.

"Mr. Decamp, here's my summer reading assignment," Devion said.

Reaching out his right hand for the paper, Mr. Decamp replied, "Good job. Actually not just a good job, great job. I know writing is hard for you and I know you struggle with it. For the rest of your life, here's a rule I want you to remember; when it comes to anything related to education, late is better than not at all. It's always better to come to class late than not at all. It's always better to hand an assignment late than not at all, and it's always better to graduate from high school late than not at all. However, late is never as good as being on time. Six months late? That's a first. Let me ask you a question. Is your paper good?"

"Yes, it is pretty good," Devion said.

"Did you cheat?" Mr. Decamp inquired. "Obviously I didn't cheat. If I was going to cheat, I would have cheated six months ago," Devion replied.

"Okay. Let's pretend that you were the teacher, and a student handed this paper to you the day it was due. What grade would you give it?"

Devion thought for a moment before saying, "It's good, but not perfect. Probably a ninety-two."

"Now take into consideration it's six months late. What grade would you give it then?"

"If I was a cool teacher or a mean teacher?"

Laughing, Mr. Decamp said, "You pick."

"I pick cool. I'd probably do six points a month times six months. That's thirty-six points off. Plus eight because it's not perfect so I'd give it a fifty-six. But fifty-six is better for my average than zero, right?"

Mr. Decamp smiled at me. From the first day of school, he preached to the kids, "Don't get zeros. Zeros will kill you in school. Thirties will not kill you. Do something. Just don't get a zero. Write part of the essay. Do a couple of test questions. Give me something." Mr. Decamp used to tell me if a teacher ever refused student work, they should be fired on the spot. The fundamental thing we do as teachers is meet kids where they are and make them better. Refusing to do that should not be tolerated. My lesson was learned.

I always take their work. My policy on late work is I don't have a policy other than I will always take it. I prefer it to be on time. If not, we will decide at that moment what's best. The reason it's late might be different depending on the student. Always be willing to change a policy or procedure the second something better presents itself. As said earlier, use words like often, usually, and frequently when creating policies. If you have a policy and want to change it, just tell the truth. "I know I said my policy on late work was minus five points per day. But I changed my mind. From now on, I'll always take your work and you will always get some credit." Now there's incentive for kids to do it. "I prefer it to be on time. If it's late, we will decide what your grade is at that time. As always, whatever is decided will be between the individual student and me, and nobody else. Sorry for the confusion." Welcome failure as a path for learning. Everything else takes care of itself.

Chapter Twenty
Mentoring, Reflecting, and Working with Parents

Today I am in McDowell County, West Virginia. According to Wikipedia, McDowell has the third lowest median household income in the country. I had a contract with them during the very early years of my consulting career. I went every month for three days at a time and worked with three different schools while I was there. It's hard to even explain what this experience was like. I'd leave my house in Rochester, New York at 4:30 p.m. I'd fly from Rochester to Atlanta, to Charleston, West Virginia. Flying into Charleston is no picnic. The airport is surrounded by mountains and the runway literally falls off a cliff. Meaning if the landing comes up short, it's over, or if you overrun taking off, it's over. I'd always give those pilots an extra nod of approval when we landed safely.

Usually by now, if everything was on time, it was about 11 p.m. I'd rent a car from Hertz, and the first night of the three, I stayed at the Hampton Inn near the Charleston Airport. By the time I got to sleep, it was usually around 1 a.m. I'd wake up around 5:30 a.m. and drive 106 miles (which took over two hours) to Welch, West Virginia in McDowell County. Now please understand this was not your normal drive. The first hour from Charleston to Beckley was perfectly fine. It was a four-lane highway. No problem. But the last hour was the most treacherous driving I've ever experienced. I'm talking about winding, mountain back hill roads. Like, legit both hands on the wheel, full grip, ten-and-two for 60 miles.

I'd work from 8 a.m. to 3 p.m. with kids and staff while school was in session, visiting classrooms, observing teachers, and talking and playing basketball with kids. Because I was there monthly, I got to know many of the high-flyers well.

I'd finish day one around 4 p.m. and drive an hour and a half to the closest hotel in Princeton. I'd get to my room around 5:30 p.m. and would go to Chili's across the street and sit at the bar by myself. I always ordered chicken fajitas with extra salsa and a huge ice water. At that point, I'd be beyond exhausted from six hours of flying, four hours of sleep, three and a half hours of intense driving, and seven hours of working with kids and teachers in one of the most impoverished places in the country. Then I'd take out my computer and type reports of all the different consult sessions, interactions, and advice from that day.

I'd get up the next morning around 6 a.m. and drive the hour and a half back to the second school, then back to Princeton. The third day, I'd drive back to Welch, work the morning at the third school, and then drive the two intense hours back to the Charleston Airport. I'd usually land back in Rochester around 11:30 p.m. that same night.

It was the most challenging and rewarding experience of my career. I personally had never seen poverty like I saw there. I'm talking about a first grade class where seventeen out of twenty-two students didn't have running water where they lived. I've worked in classes where maybe one or two didn't have running water, but never anything close to seventeen. The school was, quite literally, the only place where basic needs were ever met for certain kids. Shoutout to the superintendent (she was not the super when I consulted there), and my good friend, Carolyn Falin. Also, Amanda Fragile and Kristy East are fantastic administrators there.

During our meeting, I recommend forming a behavior committee made up of student representatives from each grade. Faculty meets with them monthly or biweekly to help set policies, rules, consequences, etc. for the school. Right now, most things are done to the kids. They're told what work to do. They're told what the consequence is. They're told where to stand in line. They're told when they get to go outside. Many are desperate to feel power and control. Committee members can include two or three of the most challenging kids from each grade level, almost like a student council for disruptive kids. Teachers try hard to focus on relationship-building, but the amount of content is overwhelming. The focus is so strong on test scores and content, that many faculty do not see and understand the direct correlation between strong relationships and higher test scores. Teachers know they should have strong relationships with students, but don't really know how to go about forming these connections. The best administrators are not afraid to teach teachers, to explain what we do well and where we struggle, and to quiz teachers about their difficult students (i.e., three interests outside of school, specifics about home lives, etc.). Encourage spending actual class time talking to kids about life and interests. You can bring in the best consultants or behavior program you want. None are effective unless kids feel like teachers genuinely enjoy being around them and want them in class.

Start a mentoring program where kids mentor each other. Have your most difficult older students mentor your most difficult younger students. This would be awesome for Ricky, whose home life is as depressing as I've ever heard, plagued with physical, sexual, and mental abuse. When he was a baby, his parents put beer in his bottle. Ms. Stillwell was amazing with him in second grade. This year, he's really struggling in third grade because the teacher isn't nearly as strong. I recommend Ricky go back to second grade to be Ms. Stillwell's class helper at least a few times per week. He loves her. She built such a strong relationship with him last year and he will be great in her room this year as the big third grade helper. Ms. Stillwell is all for it and tells me she really misses him. This also gives his third grade teacher a much needed break a few times per week.

I truly believe this will be as big a help for Ricky as it is for the kid he mentors. There's not enough time set aside for anger prevention and intervention. Kids here need to practice what to do instead of hitting. Ricky was sent to the office because he hit a student who said something about his mom. He was clearly able to articulate exactly what happened. "I'm not supposed to hit, but I got mad. I know I'm supposed to walk away and tell her I don't care what she says. And honestly, I really don't care what she says, but it's hard for me to help it."

Then he told us the next time someone does or says something like that, he will respond by walking away. Many times, Ricky is given a consequence, and everyone moves on. This time, I told Ricky we were going to practice to see if he was actually able to do what he said. I told him to pretend I was another student.

I said, "Ricky, your mom is soooooo uggggggggly!"

Instinctively he cocked his fist as if to hit me. This was directly after he just finished saying he wouldn't hit. I stopped him and said, "Okay, no good. We have to try again. Are you ready?" He nodded.

"Ricky, your mom is sooooooo ugggggglyyy!" Same response. It took us about five practice sessions before he said, "I don't care what you think about my mom," and then walked away.

Bottom line is that, if at all possible, district level administration should build time into the day for kids like Ricky to practice and role play these scenarios. See it as an investment. I'm giving up something right now to get something later.

This school has a "reflection room," where kids talk about what they did wrong, write what they'll do next time, and usually stay in during recess. The same few kids seem to be here every day. The teacher in the reflection room can practice and role play different scenarios, like I did with Ricky. I also believe there should be a reflection room for adults to write down what they did wrong, what they will do differently next time, and if taking away recess, sit with the student during that time to discuss. Arguments or power struggles take two. The adult must take responsibility for their part. "I don't like when you don't listen when I give instructions. I also need to do a better job of not correcting you in front of your friends. I'll pay closer attention to this in the future."

Improving attendance is a focal point here, as it is in most places I go. First, try to separate parents who don't care about their kid coming to school from those who don't know what to do and say when their child complains about going. The latter meaning the parent wants the kid to come, but the kid runs the show at home. Start offering monthly one-hour informational workshops to parents on different topics. This can be done in person or virtually. For example, one might wonder what to do and say when their child says he's too tired to come to school. Another parent may want to know what to do and say when their child threatens them for forcing them to school. Parents are taught exactly what to do and say in each situation. This gives them some feeling of power and control at home. Many want their child to succeed, but don't know how to help. As one parent told me a few years ago, "There's no manual that comes with getting pregnant." The goal here is to get parents and teachers on the same page. Schools with the strongest culture work with parents toward common goals. This empowers parents to do the right thing because they feel the school supports them. Parents also will meet other parents at the session dealing with the same behavior. They can talk with and consult each other. This is powerful and quickly shows which parents care to get better.

The second step is for teachers and staff to change their mentality. Negativity is rampant and many are looking for kids to mess up. This has become magnified with the birth and explosion of social media. In life, negative people are usually the loudest. On social media, their voices amplify and become one. One of the best ways to gain lots of new followers is to constantly complain about the negative parts of the profession, and we all know there are many. That said, I grew up playing sports. Maybe this is rude or disrespectful, but in the fourth quarter of a close game, I didn't want to hear my teammates complain. If someone did complain, they often got jacked up by their teammates. Focus on what you can control, your attitude and effort.

Administrators, try not to allow negative talk at staff meetings. My former principal, Beth, didn't even let us talk. I remember our first staff meeting. She walked in and said, "This is my world. I run it. Each of you run a very small country inside my world, but it's my world. Every once in a while, your country will be asked to do something for the good of the world that you don't understand, like take on a new citizen or two. You might think your borders are full, but they are not full because I see the world and just because your country had a bad day, doesn't mean I'm changing the world. Faculty meetings are my time, not yours. They are my time to tell you how the world is going to work. They are not your time to tell me how the world should work."

I remember thinking, *who the heck does this lady think she is?* Then she said, "On Monday morning and Wednesday morning, between 6 a.m. and 7 a.m., I will be in my office with the door open and the light on. That is your time to tell me how I can make this world better for your country to exist."

Why was that so brilliant? Who's going to that? Six to 7 a.m. on a Monday morning? No, thanks. I'm good. Which is exactly what she wanted. Her thought was, if it's not important enough for you to lose an hour of sleep, it's not important enough to take other people's time at a staff meeting.

I worked for Beth for three years. In three years, I set my alarm nine times and went in once. I remember waking up the other eight times thinking, "F it. It's not that important. Yesterday I cared a lot. Today, not so much." What's funny is, to this day, I know exactly what I went in for. I had just learned about rewarding everyone in honor of one and wanted to share it with her. Another thing I loved about Beth is I never worried about getting in trouble. Her rule was you were allowed to complain about anything you wanted as long as you had a solution. It was a Wednesday morning and I knocked on the door, startling her.

"Nobody ever comes, do they?" I asked.

"Not really," she said.

"I think I have a way to make the world better for everyone's country to exist," I said.

She took out a pad of paper and a pen and said, "Go."

The goal every day is to make the school and my classroom better than any other place they could be. Ask questions, and then ask follow up questions.

"How was your weekend? Where did you go? Who were you with? What time did you end up leaving? Did you stop to eat on your way home? If you could stop at any restaurant, what would you pick? What did you get? Was it good? What did you put on it?"

Connection first, every single time.

Chapter Twenty-One
Defusing Power Struggles

When a 90-mile-per-hour fastball comes from the pitcher to the catcher in baseball, there is only one way to defuse that fastball; catch it and set it down. Here it comes, at 90 miles per hour. Catch it and set it down. Some people want to hit it back. The problem with hitting it back is it goes faster, harder, and sometimes takes a bad hop and hits someone in the face. Catch it and set it down.

I was working in McAllen, Texas a few years ago, and a little old lady teacher came up to me at the end of the day. She had bright white hair and a leather-skinned face.

"I think I 'caught it' one time, but I want to know what you think," she said.

"What happened?" I asked.

"I'm going to tell you what happened, but before I do, I have to warn you. What this boy said to me is the worst thing you've ever heard a kid say to a teacher in your life. I guarantee you've never heard anything worse," she warned.

"Great. What did he say?" I inquired.

"I can't say it. It's too bad."

"If you don't say it, how am I supposed to know what he said?"

"Good point. Okay, I'm going to say it, but it is not me saying it, it is my student," she clarified.

"Lady, I gotcha," I confirmed.

"All I asked him to do was take out his books. Is that so bad?" she asked.

"I don't know. How did you ask him? Did you say please and thank you?" I wondered.

"I asked him fine."

"What did he say?"

"He turned around and said, 'I ain't taking out my books, you gonorrhea, syphilis-dripping wh*re.' Told you it was bad," she said.

"A sixth grader? Yeah, that's bad," I agreed.

"Wanna know what I said back to him?"

"I don't know. Do I?"

"Oh, you do."

"What did you say back to him?"

"Nope, not that easy."

"What's not that easy?"

"You've been 'Mr. Role Play Man' all day. Let's role play it. You will be the kid and I will be the teacher," she said.

"You want me to be the kid?" I asked. It was the end of the day, and I wasn't thinking clearly.

"Yes. You will be the kid and I will be the teacher. Go ahead, sit down." So I did. She looked at me and I looked at her, and she looked at me and I looked at her. "Go ahead," she said.

"Go ahead what?" I asked, confused.

"Call me those things."

"Lady, I live in New York. We hear stories about

Texas. Y'all kill people down here for way less than that. I'm not calling anyone anything," I said.

Then, in the God-given voice that only some teachers were given, she said, "I said, call me those names now." You know that voice I'm talking about? From the time I was a little kid, I've had a mean streak inside that I have worked hard to put away. I'm talking about counseling and therapy and addiction recovery meetings. When you want it to come out or demand that it come out, no problem. So I looked her right in the eyes and said, "Fine. I ain't taking out my books you gonorrhea, syphilis-dripping wh*re bag." I threw "bag" on the end just to leave no doubt that I am worse than any kid she's ever had.

"You want to know what I said back to him?" she asked.

"I do," I replied.

"You sure?"

"I am."

"I walked right up to that boy, and I looked him directly in the eyes and said, 'And it is exactly for all of those reasons that I am not in a very good mood today. So take out your books, now!' Is that what you meant by catching it?"

Laughing, I said, "Yes that's what I meant. What happened?"

"He looked like he had been run over by a truck. He just stood there looking at me. The whole class erupted in laughter, but for the first time all year, they laughed at something that I said instead of something that he said, and I don't care what you say, it felt so good." Agreeing with an obnoxious, defiant, or inappropriate student is such an amazing way to defuse.

It's happened to me before too. Once, a kid said, "Mr. Mendler, you're so stupid."

"Obviously, buddy. No question about it. I picked this profession, did I not? For fifty grand a year to be yelled at by you all day? Tell me how stupid I am because honestly, I didn't know it on my own," I said.

"Mr. Mendler, I hate you." A classic.

"This makes sense, because there are days I don't like myself," I replied.

Responding this way often leaves the mouthiest kid speechless. I was working in New York City in the Bronx and told that story. A teacher said to me, "I have a good one. A high school kid called me a motherf*cker right to my face. Can you believe that?"

I said, "Yeah, that's crazy. How did you respond?"

She said, "Oh, I just told him the truth. 'Well, you got it half right, but I don't have any children.' I'm not a mom but I can be the other thing. Want to see?"

Power struggles usually happen because the teacher doesn't want to look bad in front of the class and kids don't want to look bad in front of each other. One of my favorite acronyms for defusing is called LAAD, which stands for listen, acknowledge, agree, and defer.

For example, let's say a kid says to a teacher from across the room, "This lesson s*cks." Step one is accomplished. I listened. Steps two and three go together and are not easy. Acknowledge and agree. Let the student know what they are saying is or might be true. It sounds like this.

"This lesson s*cks," the student yells.

"I hear you buddy. I hear you loud and clear and I'm not even saying you're wrong. We are going to do a little math problem right now," I say.

"But I thought this was science class," they protest.

"It is, but we are going to do a little math problem. Do you know how many days there are in a normal, typical, regular school year?"

"How many, Mr. Mendler?"

"One hundred and eighty. Did you know that I teach a minimum of six lessons each of those days? Do you know what one hundred and eighty times six is? One thousand and eighty. That's how many lessons a year that I teach. Some of them are going to suck. How could they not? If you go out to eat at the same restaurant one thousand and eighty times, do you think you are going to get great food every time? I promise you won't. There might be a new chef, or they might be experimenting with different recipes. Today you got me. I don't think it was my best effort. That said, right now is not the best time for us to have this conversation. Look at the clock. When the big hand is on the two we will finish it then. Thanks for waiting. I appreciate it."

Then walk away. Notice that I thank the student before doing what I ask. Usually in the English language, "thank you" comes after someone does something. With hard-to-reach kids, it should come first. "Thanks so much for picking up that piece of paper even though I know you didn't drop it." Or, "Thanks for stopping talking. I know it isn't easy for you sometimes, but I do appreciate it."

Try this with a spouse or child as well. Call them, or even text them to say, *Thanks so much for doing the dishes, walking the dog, and getting dinner started. I appreciate it.* They'll text you back, *But I didn't do any of those things.* You respond, *I know, but thanks for doing them before I get home.* I'm not saying all of those things will be done. I'm saying it's our best shot. Work on hearing what the student says instead of how he says it. Sometimes we get so caught up in the way a message is delivered that we miss what is actually being said.

Then acknowledge it. "Frank, I hear you." When we agree with someone in this world, it's nearly impossible for them to continue arguing. "Frank, I hear you and you might be right." But then immediately defer to a later time. "If we talk about it right now, both of us will get upset and neither of us want that, so I promise we'll finish this conversation right after class or later today. Thanks for waiting."

The goal is to defer the conversation to a later time if possible. When the later time comes, begin by apologizing to the student about the role you played.

"Listen, Frank, I'm sorry. I know we both get fired up which often leads to an argument," I begin.

"I hate you. This class is so dumb," he replies.

"I know. Sometimes it is. I'm really sorry for that."

"But I can't stand—"

"I'm curious," I interrupt. "Have you ever made a mistake in your life?"

"Yes."

"When you say 'sorry,' don't you want people to forgive you?"

"Yes."

"I'm just like you. I make mistakes all the time, and obviously today I made one."

"How are we similar? You're a teacher and I'm a kid."

"I know, but I get mad sometimes and so do you. Have you ever said something, and the second it comes out, you wish you could put the words back in?"

"All the time."

"Me too. See how similar we are? I am curious, is there anything you might do differently next time? Because I definitely need to be more patient and less impulsive. What about you?"

First, I defuse the student by apologizing. Most students expect to be told what they did wrong, so this catches them off guard in a good way. I also model what I want from the student. Frequently, the conversation starts with the adult saying, "You need to do this" and, "You need to do that." The student immediately shuts down. My goal is to open up the student. Then I use questions to become their teammate by showing how similar we are. I want the student to tell me what they can do differently next time. Again, people are more likely to follow through with decisions they made for themselves than decisions others made for them. All the while, I model taking responsibility for my own actions and reiterate how I can be better in the future. It's the same process with an upset parent.

A parent might complain, "I'm not happy that you gave my daughter ten problems for homework. She's spent the last two hours working on it and only has two done. This is ridiculous."

"Ma'am I am sorry," I reply.

"But you should—" the parent starts.

"Ma'am, I said I am sorry. Have you ever made a mistake at your job? Oh yeah, you don't have a job." (Okay, don't say that last part—I got carried away).

"Well, yes."

"When you say 'sorry,' don't you want people to forgive you?"

"Yes."

"I'm no different. See how similar we are? Sometimes I make mistakes at my job, and obviously today I made one. It's never my intention for your daughter to spend two hours doing two problems. The only thing that does is get her to hate math, and I love math. Why would I want her to hate it? How many problems do you think she should have to solve tonight?"

"The two she did are enough."

"I totally agree. Let's consider tonight's homework complete with the two she did, and nothing the next two nights. Sound good?"

First, I defuse the parent by apologizing. This catches them off guard in a good way. Many parents, like their kids, expect to be told what their kid did wrong. I also model what I want from the parent. Frequently, the conversation starts with one of the sides saying, "You need to do this," or, "You need to do that," both often leading to a power struggle. Then I use questions to become a teammate first by showing how similar we are. My goal is for the parent to tell me what they can do differently next time. Again, people are more likely to follow through with decisions they make than decisions others make for them. All the while, I model taking responsibility for my own actions and reiterate how I can be better in the future.

A few other reminders to avoid power struggles. Stop needing the last word. Second to last word is best. Talk to kids as privately as possible. Get them away from their friends. Holding grudges hurts the holder most. Every day is a new day. Every hour is a new hour. If possible, every minute is a new minute. It's not personal. All of us take out frustrations on people we love and care about most. Kids are the same. Sometimes things continue to escalate with kids in class. If that happens, use the five Ws of defusing.

Say "woah" out loud so everyone can hear. Usually I believe in privacy, but sometimes things escalate beyond that. My only goal is to get the student's attention. The second she looks at me, I tell her exactly what is happening. "Woah! You and I are about to argue right now." I didn't say it was her fault. I didn't say she was to blame. I didn't say she needed to change. I didn't say she was inappropriate. You and I, together, are about to argue. Next, I explain why we are about to argue. "Woah, You and I are about to argue right now. You don't want to look bad in front of your friends and I don't want to look bad in front of the class." The good news is that it's almost always the same reason. Whether she didn't pick up a piece of paper or do her work, power struggles don't happen in private. Neither of us want to look bad in front of others. I finish by letting the student know specifically when I'm willing to discuss. This is critical. Without this piece, we leave the student hanging so it sounds like this: "Woah! You and I are about to argue right now. You don't want to look bad in front of your friends and I don't want to look bad in front of the class. I promise the second class is over, we will finish this conversation. Thank you so much for waiting. I really appreciate it."

Notice again, I thank the student before completing the task. Then walk away. As I walk away, the student might mumble under her breath. A little rain doesn't stop the airplane, and I'm the airplane. Fly through it. Many teachers stop at the first sign of turbulence; they don't give themselves a chance to get in the air. Think about an airplane when it takes off. Usually at first, there is a bit of turbulence. The plane does not slow down. Instead, it speeds up and breaks through the clouds. Often, on the other side, there is sunshine and a smooth ride.

Chapter Twenty-Two
Fun in School

I walk into a second grade room full of kids, and barely anyone notices. Usually someone blurts, "Who are you?" or, "Why are you here?" or, "Are you her husband?"

None of that happens. Instead, a few nod and the teacher continues her lesson. I notice a boy looking at me from the other side of the room. He has a striped polo shirt and shaggy hair. He gets up and starts walking over, stopping a few feet away.

Reaching his right hand out, he says, "Hi."

I shook his hand and replied, "Hi."

"My name is Chris."

"Hi, Chris."

"This is second grade math. Today we're learning about two-digit subtraction. If there's anything I can help you with, I will be sitting right over there." He points to his seat before saying, "Thanks for visiting our class."

Then he walks away. When class ends, I tell the teacher how impressed I am that someone took time to say hello to me. She tells me that at that school, every class has a greeter. Their job is to make sure any stranger walking in the room feels comfortable without the teacher getting interrupted. I tell her that I love that there's an introduction to the class, allowing me to get to know the students a bit. When I observe rooms, it's rare that the teacher stops and introduces me. I usually introduce a visitor to my class. I ask them to talk a little bit about why they're there and what they are doing. Then I allow my students to ask questions.

The teacher teaches about the different coins, and students are engaged and involved. I love a good coin rap. Penny, penny, easily spent copper, brown and worth one cent. Nickel, nickel, thick and fat, you're worth five, I know that. Dime, dime, little and thin, I'll remember you're worth ten. Quarter, quarter, big and bold, you're worth twenty-five, I'm told. JFK, you make me holler, that biggest coin's worth half a dollar.

I like that the teacher has different students come up and point to the coins pictured on the white board. Although I do caution about how they might feel if they get something wrong in front of peers. For certain kids, make sure when doing activities in front of others, they get it correct. They are taught the difference between two- and one-digit numbers. It seems easy for most of them. Never be afraid to push harder academically. With a small class and strong relationships, there is more individual attention provided, meaning that the class might be ahead of the curriculum. They have a nice room, and all of it should be utilized.

Maybe creating a reading space for kids who finish work, or a calm corner to help de-escalate situations would be a good idea. Students that are ahead (or struggling) can have a place to go within the room and not be distracted.

There is a girl that constantly needs attention. She basically attaches herself to the teacher who wants to help her, but also distracts from everyone else. We discuss the root cause of the behavior. She's desperate for attention because she gets very little at home. Clinging isn't the problem. It's the solution chosen to the problem. The goal is to figure out how to give her attention in a different way. Look for ways she can help others. I suggest choices within clearly defined limits. For example, say, "Meggie, we will be on the carpet at these five different times." This shows a limit. Continue by saying, "Please pick whichever three you prefer," (giving her a choice within the limit), "to sit right next to me. Also, please let me know where you'd like to sit the other two times we are on the carpet." Or try saying, "We will be lining up today five times. You get to be line leader twice. Which two times do you prefer? Any chance you can help in a different part of the line the other times?"

By providing choice, I take her focus off the limit. This is important for kids who look for ways to keep us in arguments. My daughter is a good example. It is well known that she loves chocolate. One of my favorite things to do when I have time in a city is to visit a local chocolate store to bring her back some. This alone has her excited for me to leave and come home. Sometimes, as many eight-year-olds do, she wants to eat too much. If I say to her, "Brookie, that's it. No more chocolate. Please put it away," she'll argue with me for one more piece.

If I say, "Brookie, no more chocolate. Quickly decide if you would prefer some strawberries, raspberries, or a banana. You can pick whatever you want. Hurry. Choose. Which do you want?" Usually she says, "I want chocolate, but I love strawberries and raspberries. Can I have both please?"

Think of it like you're driving down the road, and the second you say "no," jerk the wheel hard to the right or left, knocking the student (or in this case, my daughter) off balance. Choice is the focal point.

There are twenty problems on the page. Please pick whichever eight you think are easiest (choice). Banging on the keyboard is unacceptable. Do you prefer to do push-ups, sit-ups, or jumping jacks to release your energy? Would you like me to do them with you? Can you count or should I? Focus on offering choices and looking for places she gets to help others. Rephrase with questions instead of statements. Be careful telling a kid to calm down when they are upset. To be clear, never in the history of education have the words "calm down" actually calmed a person down. Instead of "calm down," try "what can I do to help you right now?" or "I'll give you a few minutes and come back. Do you prefer three minutes or five?"

Chapter Twenty-Three
I Was Like, "Yo"

Classroom management means I manage the only person I control at all times. Do I stay calm when he gets upset? Am I respectful to disrespectful people? Do I take the behavior personally? Am I allowing his behavior to control my emotions? Do I see it as an annoyance to deal with or a challenge to overcome?

Mr. Trist is in his first year and is upbeat about his job. The room is small and there is not much space to do labs. I immediately help rearrange the desks from rows into a "W" shape. This is not ideal, as he really does need more room. Thirty-six kids with one first-year teacher is an almost impossible task.

He has their attention from the start. He jokes with them, asks about their lives, and tells them about his. It's amazing how just a few minutes of this every day builds strong connections.

We discussed a few different kids, and I reminded him to focus on the "why" behind each behavior. Without understanding why behaviors occur, they are impossible to fix. Pretend you are a doctor, and four patients have bad runny noses. You give them all Kleenex. The runny noses go away for a bit, but all four come back the next day. After a few questions, you realize two have allergies, the third is stubborn and refuses to wear a winter hat, and the fourth is a cocaine addict. The symptom (runny nose) is the same for all, but the solution is very different.

Behavior in school is no different. What we see in the classroom from kids (calling out, head down, defiance, etc.) are symptoms of something greater. This has been written about multiple times so far.

Mr. Trist asked what to do with a student that does absolutely nothing. I told him about my former student, Ashley. It was my second year teaching, and my principal, Beth, came to my room midway through the year. Looking upset she said, "Letting you know that I have a new student for you. Her name is Ashley." When teaching self-contained and you get a new student midway through the year, it is generally not because they've done brilliantly well somewhere else. Usually, they have been kicked out or removed for some reason. Beth, looking down at four pages of notes on her clipboard, then said, "Let me tell you a little bit about her. She has been defiant, disruptive, and occasionally violent." After a few more adjectives I jumped in.

"Are you going to tell me anything good about Ashley?" I asked.

Beth scanned her sheets up and down. "Not really."

"Is she coming anyway?"

"Yes."

"Then I prefer to find out for myself," I said.

This is a rule I've adopted in my career. I prefer to

find out for myself. Each student in my class gets a fresh start. It is impossible to do this if I have a ton of information ahead of time. Beth understood, and told me Ashley would be here Monday.

I was at the door as she came flying around the corner a few minutes late. Ashley came to a skidding halt about six inches from me. My first impressions were that she was overweight. Her clothes were too tight. She wore too much makeup and smelled of cheap perfume. With her arms crossed, she looked me up and down about four times and then laughed in my face. She got closer, which I didn't realize was possible, and said, "I just wanna let you know, I ain't gonna do sh*t this year. Nothing at all. This school s*cks, this class s*cks, this room s*cks, you s*ck..." I think she even said the words, "I s*ck," which would have made no sense.

She charged into my room, brushing my shoulder upon entry and slammed herself into a desk. The desk actually tipped about half way over onto its hind legs. It slammed to the ground and there was Ashley. Now it is my job to teach her.

Every other student in my class saw and heard exactly what she said. It's not okay for them to think she can talk to me that way. I was so proud of my students because they didn't flinch. Probably because we spend a good amount of time each year focusing on prevention phrases.

"There are going to be times that some of you do and say rude, inappropriate things. When that happens (and I hope it doesn't), I might choose to walk away and keep teaching. It might look to some of you like I am ignoring behavior. Trust me, I am not ignoring it. I just think teaching those of you who are not being inappropriate is more important than stopping for the few who are in that moment." I walked directly up to Ashley, looked her right in the eyes, and said, "Nice to meet you, too." Then I walked away. Ashley was a kid that did nothing for two weeks except show up. I learned a lot the year I had her. First is that sometimes in a classroom, the teacher has no good options. Because of this, I became really comfortable picking the best of bad options. My best of bad option with Ashley; I'd always rather have a student do nothing in my room than nothing somewhere else in the building, if I see those as my only two options. If I think a student is just going to go to the nurse's office and put their head down, I'd rather have their head down in my room. Call me cocky or arrogant but when the head is down, ears still work, and I believe I'm good enough to say something to gain her interest. For two weeks, she sat in the same position, head buried in her arms on the desk. Two weeks later, we began a lesson on Hamlet.

Trying to relate the content to their lives, the assignment was to write about a time in life when you deceived someone or were deceived by someone. The next day, at the end of class, Ashley walked up to me and said, "Mr.
Mendler, I did my homework."

Before I could respond, she was gone. I went home that night and began reading the papers. I read Ben's paper first. He was with me the entire year, and his paper was well written. Then I got to Ashley's. At the time, I had no idea I'd be writing books and teaching workshops because I would have saved her paper to share. It read:

Deceivedbyashley (all one word)
There was a time in my life I was deceived it was by my boyfriend we were at a party
I was like yo what's up with that other girl
He was like yo I don't know
I was like yo what do you mean you don't know
He was like yo I said I don't know
I was like but you should know
He was like yo but I don't know

For two pages, I read, "I was like yo he was like yo I was like yo." When I got done, I was like yo! I'm not sure if you've ever been super excited to get an assignment from a student, but then totally overwhelmed at what you're seeing. That was this for me.

If I graded Ashley's paper the way many teachers do, by comparing it to Ben's paper, it would have been an "F." Some of you nicer teachers might say, "D" or "C minus," but with the long minus. If I graded Ashley's paper by comparing it to her own previous work, I would have to give it an "A." After all, it is 100% better than anything else she's done for me all year. Which decision is more likely to get Ashley to do the next assignment?

Ashley was an easy one. The first day of school, she said that she hated my class. Giving her an "F" confirms everything she already believes about English. This is the number one motivation killer of kids in school. They do the best job on assignment that they know how to do, and we tell them it stinks. I did not fall into this trap. Everyone in my room gets an "A" on their first assignment.

The next day, Ashley got her paper back and waited after class to talk to me. Without warning she said, "Do you think I'm stupid or something?"

I said, "Not at all, why would you say that?"

"Mr. Mendler, do you know how old I am?"

"Sixteen or seventeen?" I asked.

"I am seventeen years old. Just so you know, I have never once gotten an 'A' on anything in my life. This paper ain't no 'A' because I know an 'A' when I see one. So change it." At that moment, I learned she was honest. This girl was not about to steal from me. My best students never tell me their grade is too high.

"You lucked out this year," I replied

"Why?"

"Because you got me for a teacher, and you never had a teacher like me. Everyone in this class starts off with an 'A.' You can ask the other kids, but they might not remember because it was back in September. That said, has anyone ever taught you how to write a sentence? Because it doesn't really look like it."

"Not really," she admitted.

"A sentence is a subject and a verb. That's it. Nothing more, nothing less. 'Ashley runs.' That's a sentence."

"No, it's not."

"Yes, it is."

"How come they're so long in books and stuff?"

"Because there are ways to write better sentences and we will get there. I am curious. What is your favorite food?

"Why do you care?" she asked.

"I'm just wondering. If you could pick one food, what would it be?" I inquired.

"Pizza."

"I love pizza too. What do you like on top of it?

"Just cheese and sauce."

"Interesting. You like basic pizza. Cheese and sauce. Kind of like a basic sentence, subject and verb. It is possible to make the pizza better. Add pepperoni and fresh garlic. Maybe throw on some pineapple and jalapenos too. The same can be done with sentences. We can add adjectives and adverbs. We can mix in some prepositions if we want. Thing is, none of them are necessary though. All we need is cheese and sauce. Do you follow me? Tonight your homework is to write three perfect sentences."

If her sentences are perfect, her grade is an "A" again. They were not perfect. This is how low functioning of a student she was. An 11th grader is not able to complete three perfect sentences with two words.

I asked my principal, "How did she get this far in school? How is a kid who can't write basic sentences in 11th grade?"

"Ask me that again."

"How did she get this far?"

"Ask me one more time."

"How did she get this far?"

Now annoyed, Beth said, "Please don't ever ask that question again. I don't know how she got this far, but here she is. You can complain she shouldn't be here, or you can go down there and pull her up. She is way down there, so you are going to have to pull hard."

Let me take you through the next two months in a few sentences:

I ask, "Has anyone shown you how to write a paragraph? Because a paragraph is just three or four sentences put together around one topic sentence. Tonight your homework is to write one perfect paragraph. Then two, three, and four."

In the middle of May, I pointed to a white board in my room that never changed. It had the dates June 21 and 22 written on it.

"You know why those dates matter?" I asked her.

"No," Ashley replied.

"They are the dates of the New York State Regents Exam that you will pass."

"No, I won't."

"Why not?"

"Remember what I told you a few months ago about never getting an "A" on anything in my life?"

"I remember."

"I've never passed a test in my life, either. I'm always the kid who fails. I don't know how to pass tests."

"Again, you lucked out this year."

"Why?"

"Because you got me for a teacher, and you have never had a teacher like me. I don't care what the fools in Albany, New York tell you. It's not possible for you to fail. Look at what you handed me six months ago. *I was like yo, he was like yo, I was like yo*. Last night, you handed me four perfect paragraphs. You are not a failure. Remember, attitude and effort are the only two things in life people can control. You have done fantastic with both."

Then we crammed for the test. I taught her to use the words metaphor, personification, alliteration, and simile. She took the test and failed by two points. I try hard not to get emotionally tied to a student's test score, but I wanted this one badly. Ashley went to summer school, made up the two months she missed with us (remember, she came in November), and passed the second time. I've lost touch with Ashley, but my guess is if you asked her today what her best subject was in 11th grade, she would have said ELA.

With all due respect, she was not very good at English, but believed she was good. In school, this is half the battle. Kids must believe they can succeed at something before they will give maximum effort. Of course, we know this in every other aspect of life. Again, think T-ball, because we know success with the bat hitting ball comes first.

The moral of this story is, by giving kids hope, they will almost always show you effort. Once there is effort, success pops in. Once success comes, confidence takes over, and the student is officially in the cycle. Stop comparing students to each other. Instead, focus on the student being better today than yesterday.

"Yesterday, you called out inappropriately six times. Today should be five or less. Yesterday, you got out of your seat five times. Today, do you think it can be four or less? Should you keep track, or do I need to?"

Conclusion

'm going to end this book with a poem written by one of my former students, Mike. Yes, that Mike. I love poetry and we did a lot of it in my class, except we didn't do it like most teachers. My kids loved rap music but hated poetry. I wanted to teach them that that wasn't possible, since rappers and poets often write about the same things. On Monday, we did Eminem, then we'd do Langston Hughes on Tuesday. Maya Angelou on Wednesday and Snoop Dogg on Thursday. One of Langston Hughes's most famous poems is called "Mother to Son." In part, it reads:

> "Well, son, I'll tell you:
> Life for me ain't been no crystal stair.
> It's had tacks in it,
> And splinters,
> And boards torn up,
> And places with no carpet on the floor—
> Bare.
> But all the time
> I'se been a-climbin' on,"

One student said, "Mr. Mendler, what he's really saying is life has been hard. When you say one thing, but mean something else, it's figurative language."

One of Eminem's most famous songs is called "Without Me." In part, it reads:

> "The FCC won't let me be let me be
> Let me be me so let me see
> they tried to shut me down on MTV
> but it feels so empty without me."

Another student said, "Mr. Mendler, what he's really saying is when he doesn't have a song that's number one on the chart the rap industry isn't the same. He says one thing, but means something else. Isn't that figurative language?"

Without me knowing, my paraprofessional started sending these poems to student poetry contests and Mike's won first place in the "feelings" category. It also came with a check for $500 so my aide and I split it $250 each. Kidding. We gave Mike his money. He was published in a poetry book for high school kids. The only requirement for poems in my class was metaphor, personification, alliteration, and simile. Kids had to use at least two out of the four or I'd hand it right back, because New York State required those on the test. Inevitably, someone would ask if they could cuss in their poems. At first we said no but then changed it to yes, with the condition that there was no better way to say it. There is one cuss word in this poem. I will share it as is because if it was good enough for the poetry contest people, it's good enough for me. The poem is titled, "Dad, if That's What You Call It," and it goes like this:

> "Even when you're here you're never all there
> You've smoked crack so long you lost all your hair
> My friends all have fathers but I don't compare
> I've always been here and you've never been there
> You smoke your crap right in front of my face
> you ain't my father you're a f**k*ng disgrace
> not just to me but your daughter too all bad things in life
> we say are always about you
> you think you can come and go whenever you want but
> I'm not a convenience store
> I won't hold your spot. You think it's cool to live in an RV?
> You're 42 years old and still think life is one big party
> Your life's like a stinky raggedy shoe I just hope and pray
> that someday I don't turn out like you."

This is the ability some kids have that we give up on, and for what? Just because they call us a name or come a couple minutes late to class? Not in my world. Whether you love my message in this book or not is totally up to you, and I won't argue with you either way, but I hope you can't argue with the passion, energy, and belief that I bring it with. The last thing that I promise you is that your challenging, disruptive, difficult, unmotivated kids will never thank you for reading this book, so on behalf of your students, I will thank you for never giving up on **That One Kid**.

BRIAN MENDLER

BIO

Brian Mendler has extensive experience working with challenging students in general ed, self-contained, and inclusion settings. He provides staff development training for K-12 educators with the focus on how to be successful with the most difficult students. He trains thousands of educators every year and is a highly regarded dynamic speaker, podcaster & educator. Educators love his seminars, because he is able to provide strategies that work immediately for today's youth.

Mr. Mendler has recently authored a book titled, *Watch Your Mouth, Non Negotiables for Success with Toughest Kids.* The book provides educators with easy to use strategies for preventing and responding to difficult, disruptive, defiant and unmotivated behavior. He has also authored *That One Kid* and co-authored books, *Turning Tough Parents into Strong Partners, Strategies for Successful Classroom Management, Power Struggles 2nd Edition,* and the best seller *Discipline With Dignity 4th Edition.*

Please follow Brian on social media:
Twitter and Instagram @brianmendler
Facebook: /brianmendlerfanpage
YouTube: youtube.com/c/brianmendler
Podcast: The Brian Mendler Show (wherever you get podcasts)